SAVE THE DATE

Margaret —
First of all, thank
you — for the good material
to write about! This book
is supposed to help you see the
value of dating outside of marriage —
but if it helps to lead you there —
all the better!
I love you and cherish
your undying support —

Love,
Donna

Donna is the smarty pants, isn't
she? I hope you find the book
useful.

Jason King

Save the Date

A Spirituality of Dating, Love, Dinner, and the Divine

Jason King and Donna Freitas

A Crossroad Book
The Crossroad Publishing Company
New York

The Crossroad Publishing Company
481 Eighth Avenue, New York, NY 10001

Printed in the United States of America

This book is set in 11/15 Bodoni Book. The display font is Triplex.

Library of Congress Cataloging-in-Publication Data
King, Jason.
    Save the date : a spirituality of dating, love, dinner, and the divine /
Jason King and Donna Freitas.
        p.   cm.
    Includes bibliographical references.
    ISBN 0-8245-2123-4 (alk. paper)
    1. Youth – Religious life.   2. Dating (Social customs) – Religious
aspects – Christianity.   I. Freitas, Donna.   II. Title.
BV4531.3.K56 2003
241'.6765 – dc21
                                                            2003011600

1   2   3   4   5   6   7   8   9   10   08   07   06   05   04   03

To Josh and Kelly, for dating us

Contents

A Personal History

We had a lot of fun writing this book.

In the pages that follow, both immediately in this section and beyond, we talk about how dating contributes to our spiritual life and in turn how our spiritual life can give meaning and purpose to dating. Our thoughts on this topic, however, are not rooted in abstract ideas or theories but in our own experiences (which are, occasionally, rather humorous). We both have dated (though not each other), struggled with the connection between dating and spirituality, and searched and reflected on our experiences. We both also got our Ph.D.'s together in Religious Studies, and thought since we had to learn all this stuff about spirituality and religion in graduate school, we might as well put it to use for a worthy cause.

In our talk about dating and spirituality, we tell stories, we ask questions, we explore books and movies for answers and examples, we make fun of each other here and there, and we invite you, the reader, to join us in the conversation, to laugh with us and struggle with such a timely and important topic: understanding the relationship between the spiritual life and the dating life.

The essays of this particular section recount who we are as individuals in our respective dating experiences, as well as who we are together as authors of this book. We hope that our stories will introduce to you where we each come from and how we have come to embrace spirituality through dating.

Happy reading.

Why I Kissed Religion Good-bye

 Growing up I (Donna) never became particularly attached to the Christianity my parents taught me. I mostly felt nothing at all about it. I remember sitting with my dad almost every night while he read me Bible stories. This was nice mostly because I was a typical Daddy's little girl, liked to be read to, and enjoyed the attention.

I remember singing with my mom all kinds of songs about how I loved Jesus. I sang at the top of my lungs while stomping up and down the house because stomping seemed like the right thing to do given the joyfulness of the songs and since I *loved* to be loud. Also, I quickly learned that if I sang about Jesus, I had this unspoken permission to be as loud as I liked. This made the Jesus songs extremely appealing.

We went to church every Sunday and always sat right up in front. This, of course, was because I was such a hyper child and hated sitting still so much that my mom believed the only way she might get me to behave was to sit me right under the nose of the priest. When my mom taught Sunday school, I helped — mainly because then I didn't have to sit through church. Church felt like torture.

In second grade, I just about gave my mother a heart attack. We had been reading through some of the Greek myths in school — you know, sun gods and the like. Well, up until that moment I had never heard that there were even stories about other gods, never mind that some people believed in them. I didn't know there were people other than Christians.

I marched right home that day and demanded that my mother tell me about the existence of multiple gods. "Mom," I asked, "did you know about these other gods? And if so, why wasn't *I* told about them and *what if* we have picked the *wrong one?* Was God not really up there bowling during lightning storms?"

When thunder scared me when I was little, my mom used to tell me that it was God up in heaven just doing a little bowling. If the thunder was really loud, she'd say that God must have gotten a strike. Little did I know that thunderstorms were about to get a lot scarier.

You know what? She knew all about these gods and just had not told me. All that time I had been stomping around singing about Jesus, my mom had been holding out on me. She explained the whole faith thing to me at that point — that yes, there were people who believed in other gods but that we believed in the Christian God and that I needed to have faith that we were right in our beliefs. It did not even seem to concern her at all that we could be completely on the wrong side of the fence!

That was it. I informed my mom right then and there about my concerns regarding our faith. It just seemed to me that we had no way of knowing for absolute sure which god was the right god, and therefore my songs about Jesus were going to stop right then and there. I folded my arms. End of discussion. I learned later in life that there was a term for my young little struggles — I was a "precocious atheist." My poor mother!

Religion and I were a mess right from the beginning.

While these memories make me chuckle, later memories — the ones from when I started to get older are less amusing. In high school religion, Christianity and God just stopped being a struggle for me, not because all my questions were answered but because I lost interest entirely. Even though I went to a Catholic high school, I never went to church. I didn't really care at all.

I had too many other things to worry about at the time. Unlike Jason, my cowriter (don't get mad at me, J!), I was definitely *not* a geek, at least not on the outside. I was popular. It seemed that one day I woke up and suddenly all the cool guys had noticed me and wanted to take me out. I went to a million proms (but, of course, had a 10:00 p.m. curfew after them because my parents were so strict). I went to parties and dances and had this best friend I always hung out with. Life was social and life was good.

The geeky part of me, the part that led me to work hard in school and bury my head in books, I kept hidden. I cringed on honors nights when the awards I received betrayed my more thoughtful, intelligent side. Fitting in was paramount in importance. The things that did not fit in with popularity, things like religion and academic success, I pushed away.

When I went to Georgetown University, I continued my social extravaganza, at least at first. I was even a basketball cheerleader, which my friends like to joke with me about now. Religion still seemed like the furthest thing from my mind. I saw nothing of Christianity that appealed to me or my college experience. I didn't encounter anyone who was really Christian that I could relate to, and certainly none of the teaching coming my way spoke to me. Most of my friends (myself included) and the people I dated had divorced themselves from religion. It didn't seem to say anything relevant about the realities of college life, particularly relationships. Beginning from high school and continuing on into college, the most important thing people wanted to teach us with regard to Christianity was to avoid premarital sex. I learned that above all else I needed to "save myself" for marriage and just being in a room with a boy with the door shut was dangerous. Dates to the football game with friends were OK, but not anything further than that.

The lesson was loud and clear. Dating leads to sex. Sex leads to the forbidden: birth control or pregnancy, which either leads to out-of-wedlock kids or, worse, abortion. Therefore, beware dating.

As I began to mature both emotionally and intellectually, the instruction from my teachers of Christianity that "dating was dangerous" was grossly inadequate for me and other young adults around me. I didn't buy the idea that there was something wrong with dating, which I experienced as engaging, fulfilling, and significant to personal growth. This preoccupation with sex seemed silly, especially when I had so many other concerns in my life. The Christian offering of either singledom or marriage as a possible lifestyle didn't fit right. I, like my friends, was somewhere in between.

So I just tuned Christianity out altogether.

Then I discovered philosophy and everything changed. I became a self-proclaimed, all-out atheist. God is dead, I declared. (Again, my poor mother.)

My philosophy classes gripped me in a way that religion didn't. The issues I read about in philosophy books spoke to me in ways that I had been searching for. Sartre, de Beauvoir, and Nietzsche were interested in relationships, how to have "authentic" ones, and whether or not it was possible to really connect with others. However misguided I might have been in sinking my hopes for relationship guidance in existentialist philosophy (I look back with a sheepish grin now), at the time it was really all I had other than movies, TV, and all the people around me who were engaging in nightly random hookups. I needed something, and philosophy seemed like the best thing around. Philosophy excited me where religion had left me cold.

I couldn't find anything in Christianity that spoke so reflectively, probingly, and intellectually about the things that I cared about: how to navigate the relationships I encountered at college. I wanted to make meaningful choices in my interactions with others, to know who to go out with and when to get out of a relationship. I was searching for meaning in my life when everything around me was so tumultuous and fast-paced that sometimes I lost my sense of where I really was and where I needed to go. College is amazing in many ways, but it is not easy.

But it turned out that philosophy wasn't enough for me either.

What I really had needed was Christianity to grow up *with* me, and it hadn't.

How I Discovered Spirituality at Dinner One Night

 Several years later I (Donna) met someone who changed the way I look at spirituality in my relationships. I first saw Gene in one of my graduate school seminars. I remember being stunned when he walked into the room on the first day of class. First of all, he was around my age, which was exciting. (Believe me, there aren't a lot of early twentysomethings in a graduate program of religious studies). *And* he looked interesting and fun. Being a single, young, and very social person among my mostly celibate or married older peers was not always easy.

In addition to being my age, he looked like someone I had to get to know. This guy was dressed all funky — he had kind of an "irreverent grunge look" in his gas-station-attendant shirt, baggy pants, and weird shoes. On top of his basic coolness, he also had blue hair. (I later learned he changed the color each month depending on the season or relevant holiday.) He certainly brightened up my experience of that class.

It turned out that Gene lived up to his alternative look. I soon found out that he was a *juggling* youth minister and lived the life of what I would call a Christian rock star. He traveled around the country preaching the gospel while juggling and telling stories to thousands of young people. There were, and are, screaming young women (and men) everywhere he and his partner perform. Not your average Joe. Not your average Christian either.

At the time I met Gene, I guess you could have called me an irreverent Christian and a very sarcastic one at that. Yes, I was in a religious studies program, and yes, I had all kinds of questions about Meaning (with a capital M). But, what did religion, Christianity in particular, really have to say of value to my real life? Where was Christianity when I was trying to navigate the hills and valleys of life as a young person? I hadn't really encountered any satisfactory answers yet. I wanted to open my heart to faith, especially since everyone around me at graduate school seemed to find it so easy to make a commitment to this tradition that I found so irrelevant to my life. Still, that cynical attitude I had toward my Christian upbringing was always creeping back up on me.

Getting to know Gene challenged in a huge way all of my pre-conceived notions about Christianity.

From the very beginning I approached our friendship with a mixture of skepticism and intrigue. He was clearly very cool, funny, laid-back, fiercely intelligent, and just generally good to hang around with. But he had this way-out-of-proportion-Christian-commitment thing that I was not used to and had trouble figuring out. Here was someone who had not rejected religion in the way that almost everyone else I knew had. At the root of his very being was a sense of Christian spirituality that permeated everything in his life. Even the trendy stuff. A trendy, funky, *Christian* guy. Weird.

So we went back and forth constantly about religion in our friendship. I was always pestering him with questions. So if you're so Christian, what do you really think about women? What do you mean, "Preach the gospel at all times, if necessary use words"? What does the gospel really have to do with our lives and our culture? How do the young people at your shows really react to what you are telling them? Who else is out there connecting to Christianity that is our age? Why is it that you find so much meaning there and I can't?

Gene was always patiently waiting with answers (often with a wry smile). My constant questioning of his chosen lifestyle never seemed to offend him. And he certainly was more than ready to fire questions back to challenge me.

One night well into our friendship — and in the midst of bantering about favorite topics like the role of women in the church, what Christianity really has to say of relevance to unmarried people, and the pluses and minuses of coloring your hair light purple before Easter — we were having dinner at a favorite Indian restaurant in Georgetown. There was nothing particularly special about the dinner — a little curry chicken and some conversation. It was an ordinary occurrence in the context of our friendship.

Despite the ordinary circumstances, it turned out to be a very extraordinary dinner, at least for me.

Somehow over the course of a typical Gene/Donna conversation, I began wondering why I had such a strong reaction to Gene and to our friendship. What was it about our interactions that sparked in me so much curiosity, questioning, and reflecting? Why was I so challenged by another person my age who was living an integrated Christian lifestyle? And why was I fighting so hard against the challenges that Gene as a person and a friend put to me? What exactly was I struggling against?

Then it hit me. Gene had this entire *dimension* of life that was missing in my life and relationships. He had managed to allow his faith to ground his very being and everything he did; it grounded and permeated his work, his family life, his relationships and conversations. Something worked in and through Gene in all of his interactions in life. If I could draw you a picture of this, you would see Gene with some sort of glow emanating outward from him and reaching out toward everything he came into contact with, including me. That glow encircled me in the context of our friendship.

Suddenly, I wanted so badly to have that glow encircle me in more than just my friendship with Gene. I had discovered a new desire in myself. I was finally able to name a feeling that I had never quite been able to articulate before: the desire to develop and nurture a spiritual dimension in *all* of my relationships.

Over the course of a year or so, my relationship with Gene opened my heart. Through the window of our friendship, I saw how this new dimension of relating to others was so meaningful and important. I knew it had something to do with his sense of spirituality. It was as if a spiritual connection was the ground on which our entire friendship rested.

So what exactly does this experience have to do with spirituality? This is a difficult question to answer. Spirituality, to me and to many others who write about it, has to do with meaning-making. Those experiences, people, and encounters where life's ultimate meaning and our relationship to the divine suddenly shines through are what I view as spiritual. What was cool about Gene was that this sense of ultimate meaning seemed to ground everything he did. It didn't just pop up here and there. It was just a natural part of his daily life and interactions, especially his relationships.

I walked away from our conversation that evening reflecting on my other relationships, particularly my relationship with the person I was dating at the time. I wondered how to develop that spiritual dimension which I now realized was a necessary foundation to my relationships. I knew that I was beginning to feel it in my friendship with Gene, but I had no idea how to cultivate a spiritual dimension to my love life. If this spiritual dimension wasn't there when a relationship began, then how could I go about uncovering it? Did I have to create it from scratch? What if I wanted it and the other person wasn't interested? Were there some people it wasn't possible to have it with?

I felt myself shifting. It's amazing how a conversation and a little curry chicken can help a person see the world in a whole new light.

Gene and I actually never dated, but he changed the way I looked at dating forever.

When I Fell in Love in Church

I (Jason) have always been an introvert. What I thought and believed, I kept to myself. This was even truer in high school where being different often singled one out for persecution, and I was already a big enough target as it was. I liked school and played soccer in a small southern football town. Of the eighty-six people who graduated with me, around forty went to college. Of those forty, less than ten went out of state. I was one of the forty but not the ten.

I spent my university years at Berea College, a small liberal-arts school in Kentucky. Of course, being a college student, I was interested in friends, sports, and occasionally my studies. My only future plan was to get a job that did not require me to work 9 to 5 in an office.

I was pretty content. I was a decent athlete with good grades. I had an intelligent and pretty girlfriend (she is now an ER doctor). I had only one plaguing question: what was everything about?

I am not sure when this question grew to cloud my horizon or when I started reading philosophy to find an answer. I do know it was my junior year when I changed my double major of mathematics and computer science to mathematics and philosophy. I remember it well because I was so sheepish about the change. I did not tell my friends or parents. I got my advisor to sign the change-of-major form without having to explain my reasons. My only real human interaction during the change was with the gregarious philosophy professor who became my new advisor. He laughed and told me two things that put me at ease: that he was a physics major before getting his doctorate in philosophy and that any true mathematician was a philosopher. These thoughts made the transition easier for me, even though I still kept my reasons to myself. I really didn't want to have to answer the question of what one does with a philosophy degree.

Much to my surprise, my search for meaning didn't find an answer in philosophy. It found an answer through the person of Fred, a Spanish professor. "Found an answer" is perhaps too strong a phrase. Fred taught me how to search. He loaded me up with books, told me what he believed and why, and revealed to me a whole new way of looking at the world. I remember suddenly discovering that movies and novels had meaning. He pushed me to explore my Catholic upbringing. I read about the tradition I had been born into, its saints and heroes, its social and political influence, and its enormous intellectual tradition. I met people who were smart and Christian, who were Christian and good.

Still, I kept my search and my discovery to myself. I finally graduated with a double major in math and philosophy. I applied to graduate school in math and was accepted. My friends all knew I was going to graduate school. My parents thought I was going. I felt that this was where I should go too.

Instead I volunteered for a year in Chicago, teaching at an inner-city grade school.

I did not really talk over my decision with friends or family because I was ashamed of it. I felt I was being irresponsible with my education and my career. Volunteering seemed impractical, yet I knew deep down it was what I needed to do. It was what I felt called to do. I handled it as I had handled my spiritual growth up to this point — I kept it hidden so it did not distinguish me from anyone else. On the surface, I watched television, read science fiction, drank beer, and listened to heavy metal music (it was the 1980s after all). And privately I prayed, read theology, and thought about what I was going to do with my life.

While volunteering, I decided to do graduate work in religion. I applied to schools and ended up going to the Catholic University of America simply because they gave me the most money. I showed up to get my Ph.D. in religious studies and found myself in the midst of the strangest people I had ever known. They were smart but extremely socially awkward. In other words, I felt at home.

They had questions similar to mine about the purpose of creation. Some of them had answers similar to me, some had different ones, but no matter what, we were always talking about them and debating them. I was letting an element of myself that had been hidden for years become public. It was both frightening and exciting. Through this exchange of ideas and questions, these people became some of the best friends of my life. They were friends I was not only comfortable with but with whom I shared what was most important to me: my searching faith.

It was around this time that I met Kelly. I did not know quite what to make of her. She had quit her job in investment banking to do volunteer work for a year, teaching inner-city kids in Los Angeles. She had majored in economics and philosophy and was now pursuing a master's degree in religion.

A perfect fit? Hardly. While I had spent most of my life in a small town in Kentucky, she had lived in Madison, Chicago, Los Angeles, and Boston. While I disliked bars, she had some of her best times at bars. I could not dance, and she loved to dance.

What to make of her. I wasn't sure yet so I started to get to know her. It wasn't easy. I had always been awkward and was even more awkward after being in graduate school for two years. Eventually we started hanging out and soon began dating. In the beginning, neither one of us knew what we thought of the other. We had some striking similarities, but then our social habits were quite different.

Then it happened. I fell in love in church.

I used to sneak into the noon mass between my classes. I crept into the last pew and set my books down. I looked up and saw Kelly sitting two rows ahead of me.

Seeing her there made me imagine the possibility of a relationship where my spiritual journey was shared, where it was the foundation of my romantic relationship. I had never really shared my spiritual life with anyone until graduate school, and then it had only been with a close circle of friends. I had made amazing friends when I revealed this part of me. Could it be done with a girlfriend? Could it be done with Kelly? What would a relationship be like that was built on similar questions, beliefs, and values?

It was then, at that moment when I imagined the possibility, imagined what it might be like to have this kind of relationship with someone, that I fell in love with Kelly. It was not a reality but a possibility. Even now, we still work on the possibility, but it is work that is too joyful to be work.

Who would think of church as a place to fall in love? And yet, years later, it seems appropriate. I had worked to bring together two parts of myself: my public self that likes sports, beer, and television, and my private self that longs for beauty, truth, and meaning. Church also seems to bring diverse elements together: the wood, stone, and marble of the material world and the presence of God from beyond the material world. And that day at mass, these elements of creation came together for me.

I envisioned a relationship rooted in my spiritual life and fell in love with Kelly at church.

What Does a Theologian Know about Dating?

 Despite my experience of falling in love with Kelly, when I told my friends I was thinking of writing a book on dating, they asked me, "What do you know about dating?" They knew I spent most of my time reading, was awful at dancing, disliked bars, and had a Ph.D. in theology. I was more comfortable talking about first-century theologians than talking on first dates. Kelly also echoed my friends' sentiment by reminding me of my awkward and hesitant attempts to ask her out. Together they mounted a pretty good case against me offering any practical, much less meaningful, insights about dating. And, in the way only true friends can, they teased me, "Seriously, don't we already make fun of you enough? Why do something as nerdy as a book on dating? Church is already boring enough. Do you need to make dating boring too?" My initial reaction was to laugh and remember a joke about a theologian who turned wine into water as opposed to Jesus who turned water into wine. (It is pretty easy to decide whom you'd rather have at parties!) Their playful gibing did sow an element of doubt in me though. What, after all, does a theologian like me know about dating? How could I write a book on the topic?

I might have given up on the project if I had not remembered something: I have had good relationships. My first serious girl-friend, Kimmery, pushed me to imagine different possibilities for my life and to think clearly about what I believed. She dreamed of living in a big city while I had never envisioned leaving Berea. I had been raised Catholic, and while she had little religious education, she was smart, very smart. Thus she could see through any superficial answers and demanded of me reasons to explain what I believed. Since graduate school, I have been with Kelly.

She has pushed me to accept, and eventually rejoice in, who I am and what I believe in. There have been other people I have dated that have expanded my understanding of the world, strengthened my sense of self, and have made me a better person and Christian. If my theological interests were such a detriment to dating, how could I have had these good relationships?

I struggled to answer this question. Obviously there were many factors that made my relationships good: the kindness of the people I dated, loving parents, true friends, and the positive influences of works of art, books, television shows, and movies. But had theology genuinely helped me to have these good relationships? I wish I could shout "YES" without hesitation, but theology's contribution was not that clear-cut.

As a matter of fact, when I first turned to theology for answers to my questions on dating, I found it a hindrance. There were theologians who wrote on marriage, sexuality, and love, yet as these authors praised marriage, they portrayed dating as an unfortunate step toward marriage. As they detailed the beauty and joy of sexuality in marriage, they disparaged dating as leading to sexual sins. They talked of the perfect love of God for his people, the sacrificial love of Christ for his Church, and the sacramental love of wife and husband, but no word was given to the love shown between two people dating.

But this turned out not to be the whole picture. Beneath the surface of these condemnations were invaluable insights on love and relationships. The authors who dismissed dating also talked about the need for companionship and friendship to shape one's character and beliefs. I thought to myself that dating might be considered a type of friendship and hence contribute to my moral and Christian life. These authors wrote about how love for a particular individual prepared us to love the neighbor. I began to interpret dating as a particular practice in loving, not quite friendship, yet not quite marriage either. These authors stated the need to understand marriage as part of the meaning and purpose of creation, as part of the Christian story. I started viewing dating as at least compatible with the Christian message and thinking that it might be a way by which people fulfill Jesus' command to love God and neighbor.

So theology helped me in my relationships. It provided a deeper meaning to dating and made me see the possibilities that it opened up for me, yet it had done so in such a subtle way that I almost hadn't noticed. Still, for this to happen, I had to ignore the condemnations and reinterpret the insights to fit with dating, and this had taken me many years to do. Even then my theological understanding of dating was incomplete and full of holes.

Still, theology had helped me, and I was content with what I learned — that is, until I found other people struggling with dating. I worked in college and high school residence halls for several years and taught college and high school students even longer. When I had the good fortune of talking with or teaching students about relationships and love, I noticed a strong desire in them to know what dating was about, how it fit in their lives, how they could have good relationships, and what they should and should not do on dates. How could I help them? I had struggled for years with these issues myself, and while theology had helped me, I had had to learn what to take and what to leave behind, and had endured six years of graduate school to be able to do so. This is not your average spiritual journey and not a typical path for most people struggling with relationships.

I initially started to assist others by leading them down the same road I took, pointing out books that had been crucial in the development of my thinking, but I always had to preface these books with warnings about the negative attitudes toward dating and the need to look for the underlying insights. I quickly realized that this approach would take them almost as long as it took me. By then, they would probably be done with dating.

How could I get them to the good material without having to go through the bad?

I did what any good theologian would do. I wrote a paper with Donna on dating and presented it at a conference to see what people thought. There we found students, professors, elderly couples, widows, and same-sex couples who were interested in the topic. Some agreed with what we had to say. Others disagreed. Several suggested changes or other topics that needed addressing. What struck me most of all, though, was how many people were searching for something intelligent and meaningful about dating relationships. In light of these needs, we also realized that our paper was inadequate.

And that was when we came up with the idea for a book on dating. It would be a book built on what we had learned from theology and spirituality, and it would try to address many of the questions that people had about dating.

At this point I had to laugh because my friends had teased me about not having anything to say about dating because of my theology background, and it was precisely this background that had provided Donna and me with something to say. As a matter of fact, it provided us with a whole book of stuff to say!

The Essential Reader's Guide to *Save the Date*

 You may have already guessed from our initial essays that we (Jason and Donna) are in different places in our relationships to spirituality and Christianity. We each offer a relatively distinct perspective on religion in this book. Sometimes, though, our voices on a subject are so similar that even we cannot hear the differences. Essays like "Why TV Makes Us Laugh (and Cringe) at Dating" and "We All

Want Movie Love" are good examples. Yet at other times, the language and interest of one of us is more prominent than the other in a particular essay.

For me (Jason), there are a few essays where my viewpoints come out strongly. The clearest are "Dating Strengthens our Spiritual Life" and "The Value of Kissing." Yet, to find my voice, you do not need to hunt down particular essays. My voice comes out in quotations from scripture, new and old theologians, or, occasionally, contemporary novels.

My background is Christian and has always been Christian. Both of my parents were Christian and went to church every Sunday, but beyond that, and sometimes I think more importantly, my parents were good and loving people. Their Christian beliefs manifested themselves in good, loving, and just actions. When I did wrong, I was addressed as an adult. My family would talk over the issue, and we would come to a decision about what was a fair punishment. When I did well, my parents were there to praise me and encourage these actions. What I grew up in was not just a Christian family but a Christian family whose beliefs were manifested in every one of its actions. It was a Christianity I could not help but believe in. Because of this background, you find my interests in and my need to connect what I say to the scriptures.

Granted, I did have my questions along the way — serious questions. I liked thinking and reading, and occasionally I would read material that would challenge what I thought. My parents, while always good to me, could not always provide answers. I searched, questioned, and doubted, especially when I got to college. There, though, I ran into several professors and one in particular, who were intelligent Christians. They introduced me to the two-thousand year intellectual history of Christianity. Within this history, I was able to find great minds who struggled with similar questions and who provided answers that I could reflect on. Because of these influences, I enjoyed the intellectual enterprise and found great help in theologians, new and old. Thus, you find these resources scattered throughout the book.

Along with this background, I am also an avid participant in pop culture. I enjoy television, go to the movies regularly, and read as many books as I can get my hands on. I used to think of these interests as separate from my Christian faith but eventually realized quickly that they help me understand what I believe in, sometimes as an example, other times as new insights, and still at other times as something I know to be false. I also find that I share these interests with lots of other people, so they have become an important means for connecting with students in my teaching. Thus, many of the fictional stories scattered throughout these essays are there because I find them not only helpful with my faith but also because other people really enjoy them.

In this book then, essays that are more explicitly Christian usually come from my perspective. But, for those of you who are Christian reading this book, don't discount Donna's influence on these essays. She has helped to refine and expand my thoughts with questions, ideas, and sources with which I was unfamiliar. I hope I do the same for the essays that are more from her perspective. When you find a scripture quotation or a theologian introduced in an essay that does not seem explicitly Christian, it is my attempt to show that the ideas in the quotations or in the theologian's thought are intimately connected to Christianity, even if they don't seem to be on the surface.

As you already know, I (Donna) differ from Jason. I am someone who, for most of my life and at times even still, has "kissed religion good-bye." While growing up, I did not believe what I was told about who I should be and what I should do according to the Christian church. Who I felt I really was and thought I should become as well as what seemed right in life given the values and beliefs I was developing about love, relationships, and truth led me away from any recognizable connection to Christianity and spirituality. I just forgot about religion. It became a non-issue for me.

Since college, and my atheist-declaring years, I have been one of those people declaring myself "spiritual but not religious." I have had an extremely bumpy relationship with Christianity so sometimes when I read the word *Christian* I find myself feeling left out. Often the Bible does not resonate at all with me. I cannot lie and tell you here that the Gospels have held a huge influence throughout my young life because they have not. In my graduate classes in religious studies, I was known to ask fellow peers and professors to explain "this whole Jesus thing" to me. I just did not get it nor did I understand what the big deal was all about. Even today I can not stop trying to understand because in many ways I want to feel what everyone else feels. I do not want to be left out all of the time. Rejecting Christianity altogether does not feel quite right to me anymore, yet I have yet to find the place where I fit.

I am that spiritual person struggling to figure out if her sense of spirituality may be adequately expressed within the context of Christianity. I am still unsure of the answer, but in the last several years the hole created in my life by not affiliating myself with a spiritual community has led me to open up the door to Christianity again, if only little by little, to see what I might find. Though I know that some of you cringe at this admission, I'm also convinced that others of you nod your heads because you relate to what I am saying. You either are or have been in a similar place.

We write not only for people who know where they stand about spirituality and Christianity in terms of membership within the institutional church, but also for people who are uneasy about what their relationship to religion and spirituality is. If you find yourself in what I say, know that I too stumble over some of the Christian language used in this book. I also struggle in my attempts to identify with the biblical references. Yet both the language and the references are here because Jason and I believe that our ability to set the concerns of our young lives in the context of spirituality *and* Christianity (if that is the tradition you grew up with too) is undeniably important. You should not have to throw your religious heritage out the door because you, as was my experience, can't find your concerns or yourself represented within it. I *have* been nurtured by Christianity in many ways, though I do not always admit this publicly. (I'm sure Jason is chuckling knowingly right now as I confess this.) Only recently have I begun to realize that, like it or not, I have gained something important from growing up with Christianity.

So here I am writing this book.

And it follows that while the particularly "Christian" essays are more influenced by Jason, the more "spiritual" essays, such as "Making Dating Meaningful," "Spiritual Intimacy," and "Dating Shipwrecks Us" are written more from my perspective (though on all the essays we ultimately worked together).

Jason and I hope to show you that both spirituality *and* the tradition you grew up with are not just about a set of rules and regulations you have to follow. People today (myself included at times) seem to think that by being spiritual and not religious, you do not have to worry about dealing with any rules or values you do not like. Yet by approaching spirituality *and* religion with openness, I believe that through *both* we can learn about who we are as individuals within a shared community. It is possible both to develop a sense of what it means to love *and* to find out how to be a young person who finds a place in religion, without sacrificing connections to the contemporary world.

For us (Jason and Donna), the differences in our perspectives are not a detriment to the book. Instead, we believe they are one of its greatest strengths. Struggling with how we are differ-ent, challenging each other in our thinking, and shedding light on particular issues for each other has been foundational to our friendship. We have talked and talked and talked, disagreed, agreed, and compromised at different points in both our friendship and in what we say about dating and spirituality. As a result, the book is written both for Christians who have serious questions stemming from their faith and for people uncomfortable with Christianity but who still have an intense interest in spirituality.

We suspect that you as readers will identify with one of us more than the other. Some of you may identify with Jason, who has remained steadfastly committed to Christianity throughout his life, though not without struggles to understand what it means to be a good, young Christian in a culture that does not seem to support Christian values. Others of you will relate better to Donna, who rejected Christianity altogether for most of her young adult life and is struggling to understand her relationship to spirituality and how spirituality fits in, if at all, to the religion with which she grew up. We hope our differences will give you, the reader, a greater chance of finding yourself represented in the pages that follow.

"Reality" Dating

We admit that we are both pop-culture junkies.

We watch TV, go to the movies all the time, hang out at book-store cafés, and surf the Internet like everybody else our age. We also can often be found playing Play Station, though we perhaps prefer different games. We are immersed in the culture around us and we like it.

Through this culture, we learn what is important and valuable in the world, and it is through culture that we also often find out about dating. Through television shows, movies, books, and computers, we can learn what people and our culture in general think about dating, what it is supposed to be, and how to succeed at it. So naturally we went looking for love in these resources with great expectation. Unfortunately, though, these resources proved to be of little help, though they gave us some good laughs.

The understanding of dating that we gain through pop culture is not exactly wrong or bad, but rather incomplete. It looks at the funny or awkward side of dating but doesn't look for any deeper meaning in it. Technology helps us to stay in touch with friends far away but separates us physically and emotionally. Movies may capture the heights of love but fail to capture its essence. The books we found in the relationships section of bookstores were hilarious but disturbing, and television left us with similar reactions.

The following section grows out of our conversations on the different dimensions of pop culture. We decided to title this section "'Reality' Dating"; given the *Survivor* culture of our day, we're sure you can guess why.

Why TV Makes Us Laugh (and Cringe) at Dating

There are a lot of television shows on dating. Originally there was *The Dating Game*. In recent times, we've had such shows as *Elimidate*, where you get rid of one of the several suitors on your date; *Blind Date*, where the show films a blind date and makes sarcastic comments about it during the broadcast; and *Change of Heart*, where each member of a couple goes on a date with another person to see if he or she wants to stay in or leave the current relationship. These seem tame compared to *Joe Millionaire, Meet the Parents,* and *The Bachelor* variety of TV-dating/find-your-soulmate shows, where participants are often reduced to hysterics or to lounging half-naked in hot tubs. All of these shows are courtesy of the wildly successful "reality TV" industry that fascinates us these days and that is designed, we think, to make us cringe about the ups, downs, and rejections that are part of dating.

In addition to the reality shows specifically about dating, there are the sitcoms. We have shows like *Friends* and *That 70's Show*. While they are not specifically about dating, each frequently uses dating as a means of developing characters and getting laughs. *Friends* often shows us the foibles of dating for the twenty-something generation. When *That 70's Show* depicts dating, it tries to picture it the way it was in the 1970s, the decade that followed on the heels of the 1960s "free love" era.

One of our favorite and most telling story lines is the Rachel and Ross saga from *Friends*. It began many years ago when Ross had a crush on Rachel. When Rachel reentered Monica's life, Ross finally got up the courage to ask her out. They began to date. Rachel, though, got scared, broke up with Ross, but returned the next day saying she made a mistake. In the meantime, however, Ross had (already!?) slept with another woman. This brings their relationship to an end with Ross claiming that they "were broken up."

Ross wanted Rachel to come back to him, but Rachel refused for a long time. Finally Ross moved on and fell in love with Emily. As Ross got closer to Emily, Rachel's feelings for Ross became stronger. Eventually Rachel flew to England, where Ross was to marry Emily, to tell Ross about her love. She arrived just before Ross and Emily's wedding but was afraid to tell Ross. Ross, however, said Rachel's name instead of Emily's during the marital vows. Whoops. This started the marriage off badly as anyone could imagine, and, eventually, it ends.

Ross and Rachel still did not get back together. They danced around the idea until their romantic interest in each other faded into the background of the show (except for a quick marriage in Las Vegas under the influence of alcohol). This quiet situation erupted again when Rachel found out she was pregnant with Ross's baby (after a one-night foray). Joey announced his love for Rachel (the plot thickened), and then Ross and Rachel thought about getting back together.

Quite the dating adventure!

Perhaps this is an excessive retelling of a plotline that everyone seems to know already, but we think it is necessary to make a point. The Ross and Rachel relationship has to continually get more and more outrageous to be funny. In the beginning, it is enough for the two to just be going out. First dates are funny enough as they are, but eventually you have to add some conflict. Rachel is scared. Ross sleeps with someone else. Eventually the initial humor wanes, so you have to add even more drama to get the same amount of laughs you had before. Thus, Ross and Rachel love each other one week and hate each other the next. They get drunk and get married. Then, they get sober and get divorced.

They sleep together. They have a baby. They think about getting back together.

The Ross-Rachel relationship is not meant to address moral dilemmas or offer a realistic perspective of dating. Rather *Friends* uses Ross and Rachel to get laughs. The writers and producers have to continually escalate the conflict in the relationship to get more laughs. Why? Getting laughs is their business. It is how the show gets ratings, sponsors, and, thus, earns money.

Like *Friends*, all the shows we've mentioned were created as entertainment. The reality dating/try-to-find-a-soul-mate shows generate conflict in relationships in order to entertain, to cause laughter, but also sometimes to shock and humiliate. Sitcoms are *situation* comedies. They put people into situations to generate laughs. *Their whole purpose is to make us laugh.*

In eighth grade, I (Jason) was not reflective about my television viewing. I watched TV avidly and knew the TV guide well. My favorite shows were sitcoms. I watched *M.A.S.H.*, *Night Court*, and *Cheers* regularly. I enjoyed them and didn't think too much about them. At least, I didn't think about them until I decided to break up with my eighth-grade girlfriend. We had dated for a few months, the magic was gone, and I wanted to break up. How did I do it? I just stopped talking to her. I did not tell her I wanted to break up. I just stopped talking to her and hanging around her altogether. (Some of us today, no longer eighth graders, still seem to believe this is an appropriate way of ending a relationship. Ahem. You know who you are.)

As you can imagine, this approach did not go over well with the girl. It hurt her feelings a lot. Reflecting on this now makes me realize how immature I was at that point in my life. Why had I behaved this way?

There were many factors involved (like the fact that I was in eighth grade) but one of them was the assumption that everything would turn out OK in the end no matter what. I had unconsciously picked up this principle from watching television. All of the sitcoms were resolved in half an hour, and there was no tension left over the following week. I too would be free of this tension, right?

TV lied to me!

Actually, this is not true. The problem was that I assumed that television was telling me something about the world when all it was trying to do was make me laugh. I had relied on television too much, especially for understanding dating.

Television often makes dating either way too messy (e.g., Ross and Rachel) yet always all right in the end, or way too disturbing (e.g., reality TV). Allowing television to be a major source in shaping our understanding of dating relationships ultimately skews and diminishes our notion of what dating is all about. We learn to believe dating must either be filled with humorous drama or extreme tension, along with lots of sex, and the constant potential for humiliation and rejection.

So when we watch television, we shouldn't be expecting too much help in understanding relationships. We might learn to laugh at our own awkward situations and face our relationships a little more lightheartedly. We may also continue to cringe as reality TV gets scarier and hope that its "reality" claim is unfounded in our own lives. Ultimately we should remember that television is not trying to *teach* us about real life and relationships. It is designed to make us laugh and sometime cringe. In "real life," it is important for us to remember that getting drunk and married or ending a relationship by not talking or calling anymore is no laughing matter.

No matter what we do or how hard we try, we should not try to be Ross and Rachel (though they do seem to have a lot of fun). And we should especially try not to end up on shows like *Joe Millionaire!*

We All Want Movie Love

Sigh. Big sigh. This is the sound we make as we leave movie theaters after seeing a romantic film. Ah, love. If only we could be Julia Roberts and Hugh Grant in *Notting Hill,* Julia Stiles and Heath Ledger in *Ten Things I Hate about You,* or Meg Ryan and Tom Hanks in *You've Got Mail.* Life would be perfect if only we could be dating Reese Witherspoon. Or, if Freddie Prinz Jr. would only turn our way, we would want for nothing else.

And we keep dreaming.

Movie love is a dreamy kind of love. It reveals to us in two hours brief moments of loving and dramatic exchanges between two (usually beautiful) people.

Movie love is like intense romantic interludes or the kind of love we hear about in fairy tales. Fairy-tale love is great too. It keeps us fascinated. We can't get enough of this type of romance. It makes us want the same kind of experience in our own lives.

The thing is, though, and you have heard this before of course, movie love is pretty misleading. Fairy tales are rare. It is not often that a United States senator falls in love with a Manhattan hotel chambermaid as in the movie *Maid in Manhattan.* That is unless the maid happens to be J. Lo. Crazy-famous movie stars do not frequently fall in love with nondescript guys who spill coffee on them — that is, unless the guy is Hugh Grant.

Oh, why don't these things happen to all of us?

What is wonderful about movie love is that it makes us sigh. In the darkness as we absent-mindedly reach for our popcorn, the movies give us glimpses of the wonder that love and romance can be in our lives. We may not be Freddie Prinz Jr., Ben Affleck, or Gwyneth Paltrow, but that doesn't mean that there won't ever be someone who comes into our lives and sweeps us off our feet. It doesn't preclude us from one day waking up and realizing that the boy- or girl-next-door, or even better, the best friend we have had for what seems like a lifetime, is pretty much the dreamiest person in the world.

These types of experiences really do happen. That is why there are movies about them. They are some of the most wonderful and memorable experiences that life has to offer us.

And yes, these are also the types of experiences that can happen when we date. The exciting feelings we carry around with us when we realize we like someone a lot and that person likes us back are *wonderful* feelings. Those same wonderful feelings keep us glued to our seats and going back again and again to all the movies that allow us to live or relive the amazing moments of romance at the beginning of relationships.

The Bible has its own version of movie love: the Song of Songs. It expresses that awe-inspiring, all-encompassing, excitement about another person — the kind of love that enraptures us: "On my bed at night I sought him whom my heart loves — I sought him but did not find him. I will rise then and go about the city; in the streets and crossings I will seek him whom my heart loves. I sought him but I did not find him. The watchmen came upon me, as they made their rounds of the city: Have you seen him whom my heart loves?" (Song of Songs 3:1–3)

Will she meet her lover? Will they not find each other? Will they be subject to a seemingly endless number of near misses where they almost find each other but then something or someone gets in the way holding them back from blissful love? Will there be a satisfying ending where we walk away happy that love and bliss are found at last?

Granted, the Song of Songs is not a movie. It's poetry. Yet it allows its readers a glimpse of the passionate, longing side of love, much as a movie does. In the Song of Songs, we become spectators watching, reading the story of two people who are discovering the beginning of love's joys, the feeling that one's whole world is wrapped up in the object of love.

Back up a minute though. A couple of moments ago, we mentioned that one of the reasons why we get so addicted to movies about romance is that they allow us to relive those amazing moments at the beginning of relationships. What we need to remember when we go to the movies is the word *beginning*. Movies often lull us into forgetting — not maliciously, but still it happens — that romantic movies usually only give us glimpses into beginnings. And beginnings are often the most exciting part of relationships. Beginnings involve the moments that really grip us, when we can't think about anything or anyone else because we get so wrapped up in this one other person. Beginnings are fun but often not the most productive part of life or relationships.

Movie love is mostly about discovery. It is certainly possible and even hopeful that at some point in our lives we will meet someone who we will continue to take joy in discovering for an entire lifetime. Yet the discovery we experience vicariously in the movies is the very beginning kind, which is also often the most intense. No matter what movie love feels like or makes us do, it can never endure, and we should not be deceived into thinking that dating relationships can (or should) always be like relationships in the movies. Discovery can be extremely exciting — the discovery of another person, his or her likes, dislikes, who he or she is, what he or she brings out in us and makes us feel, is one of the best parts of dating. Yet this process of discovery can also sometimes capture us in an extreme and unhealthy way, to the point that we cannot think about or do anything else. Or, we can get so wrapped up in the excitement of the very beginnings of discovery, that when the "beginning" part wanes, we lose interest in the other person. Or, somehow we feel deceived by a relationship that at one point seemed so wonderful and amazing but now seems boring in comparison.

These are some of the pitfalls of hoping for movie love.

Of course, the other thing that movies seem to want to convince us about regarding dating and love is that sex is a central part of the beginnings of love. (It's the same thing with television shows.) He/she likes me. I like him/her. We hop into bed together, right? Discovering you like someone is also about seeing whether or not you can have great sex right away. Having sex is part of how we determine whether or not we are in a relationship, right? Movies confuse dating with sex all the time. (Religion does too; we'll discuss that more later on.)

What's dangerous about love in the movies is that it can deceive us and make us believe that all our experiences of love should be all encompassing, death defying, quirky, sweet, romantic, and Meg Ryan-esque. Movies seem to want to convince us that the fun and exciting beginning moments when we discover we are in love *are love* in its entirety. They often want to convince us that sex is what dating love is all about. Yet dating relationships are about much more than this. They involve a process of discovery that can last a lifetime, or just a short time, because our experiences of discovering another person can be so much more than those exciting beginnings.

As you can tell, our feelings about the movies and what they tell us about dating and love are mixed. We both *love* going to the movies and have gone to many together. We talk about the movies and what we learn about love when we go. We sigh and laugh and cry (Jason cries a lot especially) and get frustrated and angry by what we see. No matter what, though, we always go back.

After all, the more movie love, the better. Big sigh.

"I Love You," Double-Click

 Our grandparents communicated through personal encounters and letters. Our parents had telephones. We have the wonderful new technology of the Internet, especially e-mail and Instant Messenger (IM). And we *do* mean it is wonderful. It is extremely fast and reliable (most of the time). We are able to contact people at all hours of the day and night, and in all parts of the country. Both of us keep in touch with friends in South Dakota, New York, Toledo, Washington, D.C., and even Denmark. We were able to work together on this book because of e-mail. Almost every essay was started by one of us, e-mailed to the other one for revision, e-mailed back for a final check over, and then submitted to the publisher, again via e-mail.

Technology makes the communication of information so much easier.

But — and you know there had to be a "but" — the technology also can have unintended consequences. One is a distancing of the self from others. Sure, we can keep up with by friends over e-mail, but this communication is different than seeing them in person. We can have a conversation over IM, but the software cannot capture the inflection of our voice and the expressions of our faces that oftentimes carry so much of the meaning. With regard to dating, "I love you" is now frequently followed by a mouse-click to send off the message instead of the hug or the kiss that traditionally followed the phrase. Our sentiments are becoming disconnected from our bodies. Even "I love you" on the phone is disconnected, though you can at least hear the person's voice on the other end of the line.

A high school teacher gave us a disconcerting example of how technology creates this distancing. She taught at an all-girls school and told us how her students got together with guys. A friend would put a boy and girl in touch with each other through IM. The two would proceed to converse on-line about a variety of topics and, if the virtual conversation went well, would set up a time to meet at some neutral location, usually a party. There they might talk, but usually they would just make out. Later that evening, they would return home and talk to each other over IM again. This would continue until either one party became uninterested or one party phoned the other. The phone call was the sign that the two had started a serious relationship.

What?

Perhaps the most disconcerting part of the whole process was the girls admitting that they said things on-line that they would never say in person or even on the phone. They were fully aware that the self they portrayed through IM was not an accurate picture of who they were. The technology made deception extremely easy.

We don't know if this is your experience. We don't even know how common this experience is. The fact that it happens, however, shows how technology can cause you to become disconnected from other people and the world. The example above is disturbing in two aspects. First, e-mail and IM seemed to create forums where students were more at ease saying things they would not say in public and even portraying themselves in ways they normally would not. Second, and perhaps more significant, the students seemed to move from IM to kissing and other sexual activity without feeling the need to go through in-person conversations or dates. Sexual expression is divorced from personal (as opposed to virtual) relationships implying that we can use others just for sex, without caring or bothering to get to know the person we are "knowing" (if you know what we mean).

This phenomenon reminds us of a religion that emerged around the same time as Christianity. This group was called the Gnostics. The Gnostics believed that the human spirit was good but that the body was, at best, irrelevant and, at worst, evil. Some Gnostics called people to reject this world and practice heavy fasting and self-discipline. Others argued that since only the spirit mattered, you could do whatever you liked with the body. You could fast heavily or eat a lot; you could be celibate or have as much sex as you desired. The body, our physical self, was totally disconnected from and did not affect the spiritual self.

Christianity took a stand against Gnosticism. It insisted not only that the body was good — remember God took on a body — but that the body is connected to our spiritual life. C. S. Lewis captures this Christian valuing of the body in his book *The Screwtape Letters*. The book is a series of letters written by Screwtape, a devil, to his nephew Wormwood, another devil, on how to corrupt humans. In one letter, Screwtape advises Wormwood to not allow human beings to think about the connection between their bodies and souls. Screwtape writes, "for they [human beings] constantly forget, what you must always remember, that they are animals and that whatever their bodies do affects their soul."[1] In other words, the body is essential both to who we are and to our spiritual selves.

The danger of separating our spiritual life from our physical life is why the IM example concerns us. E-mail and IM can create an impression that the body and physical interactions are unimportant or even irrelevant to who we are as whole persons. It is easy to conclude that there are no consequences for maintaining relationships only through e-mail, thus divorcing our sexuality from our spirituality, and separating dating from our values and beliefs. We substitute the computer screen and typewritten words for the presence of and interaction with others. It seems simpler that way.

We double-click instead of gaze into each other's eyes.

All right, perhaps this is a bit of an exaggeration. We don't want to insist that this will happen, that all of us will carry out the entirety of our dating relationships minus the sexuality part over the Internet. Nor are we saying that e-mail, the Internet, and dating can't have a positive side.

Our friend Margaret, for example, knows the positive side. She's been having a lot of dates lately.

A while back when Margaret and I (Donna) were catching up on our respective lives, I asked her what she was up to. She told me that one day that week she was going out to hit golf balls during her lunch break. Mind you, Margaret had never touched a golf club in her life. A couple of days earlier she had gone out on a date with this rock-climber man. The golf-ball-hitting lunch break turned out to be with another guy she had recently met — he'd suggested golfing as an alternative to dinner or coffee. In addition, in the last couple of weeks she had gone out on several other dates with some other pretty cool, nice guys. These were real dates too — dinners, movies, conversation. There was no meeting at a post-IM party and going home separately after a make-out session.

So where was Margaret hanging out and finding all of these people so that she never seemed to have a dull moment on the weekends (or apparently during her lunch break either)?

The Internet. An Internet dating service to be specific. Go, Margaret!

Margaret had started a subscription to one of the many on-line dating services, which allow you to select people off their website that you would like to meet. Subscribers maintain mail-boxes where people who want to date can get in touch. All of this communication, at least initially, happens by e-mail.

Through this on-line dating service, Margaret was meeting all kinds of people. She was going out on lots of nice dates, getting to know people who shared her interests, and even finding people to set her friends up with too. So far, she had not met the man of her dreams, but she was enjoying the opportunity to connect with new people.

So are we advocating that to find dates you should go sign up for an Internet dating service? No. All we are pointing out is that, in addition to e-mail being convenient for us all keeping in touch, something like an on-line dating service (which a lot of us like to laugh at) can be a positive way for people with similar interests and beliefs to get in touch — and sometimes meet the person of their dreams. (We have a few Jewish friends who have met and found their life-long partners from some popular Jewish dating sites.) What works and is fun for some people is not meant for everyone.

The thing to remember about Margaret and her use of the Internet to find dates is that she actually went out on real dates. She did not start IM relationships or e-mail-only correspondence with people. If she found someone interesting and they found her interesting too, they set up a time to get together, sit down face to face, and have some conversation. They did something fun together — they ate, hit golf balls, went rock climbing, or whatever sounded right. Once the decision was made to meet, the correspondence over e-mail moved forward to talking on the phone and then in person. The interaction became human rather than technological.

Thus, the double-click is never enough. E-mail, the Internet, and IM must always be seen as helping us to stay in touch with those we cannot communicate with in person. If we lose sight of this role of technology, we run the risk of separating ourselves from direct human contact. We might devalue the connection between our sense of spirituality and human interaction, between spirituality and our bodies.

We must remember that no matter what, the double-click is no replacement for human affection and face-to-face interaction.

A Worst-Case Scenario Survival Guide

 We've tried television, the movies, and the Internet in our looking for love and understanding in dating. So what about books? We both love to read. From fantasy to politics to theology, we read. It was natural for us, then, in reflecting on dating and spirituality, to also search the bookstores to see what books might have to say.

What we discovered was both comical and problematic. We had to look for books on dating in the "self-help" section or in a "relationship" section located next to the "self-help" one. When we found them, the most popular books had titles like *Building a Better Spouse Trap; The Complete Idiot's Guide to Dating; Dating for Dummies; The Rules; Men Are from Mars, Women Are from Venus;* and, of course, *The Worst-Case Scenario Survival Handbook: Dating and Sex.*

What made us laugh were the titles. Our favorite was the *Spouse Trap.* It is hard not to appreciate a good pun. Some of our friends liked *Dating for Dummies.* They had a few people in mind that they felt could benefit greatly from such a book. Others liked *The Rules.* The book's 1950s view of dating seemed comical to those of us that believed in the equality, intelligence, and dignity of women.

Still, these laughs about the title couldn't make up for the distorted understanding of dating we found inside (especially with books like *The Rules*). These books do not start with the purpose, end, or meaning of relationships. Neither do they consider the human need for relationships or the joy that often springs from them. Instead, they all seem to agree on and begin with the premise that dating is a problem in need of fixing.

The *Dummy* and *Idiot* series are written as guides to solve a problem: acquiring knowledge that you should have. Hence, there are *Dummy* and *Idiot* guides for computers, job hunting, car maintenance, and, of course, dating and relationships. While humorous, *The Worst-Case Survival Handbook* seems to try and give genuinely practical advice. One assumes from the title that this advice is important in the life-and-death struggle of dating. Even John Gray's highly popular *Men Are from Mars, Women Are from Venus* is subtitled *A Practical Guide for Getting What You Want*. Dating is problematic, in Gray's opinion, because people seem unable to get what they desire in relationships or are unable to acquire relationships at all.

These books claim to identify for us false "myths" and "stories" about dating. In *Relationships for Dummies*, Dr. Wachs, the author, rejects as false such myths as "Love at first sight," "I've found my soul mate," and "If I find my perfect partner, I will be perfect and saved." According to Ellen Fein and Sherrie Schneider in their *The Rules: Time Tested Secrets for Capturing the Heart of Mr. Right*, the myth that needs dispelling is that women *should* dispense with the understanding of dating and marriage as a game of catch. Dating and marriage, they maintain, are indeed just that.

While the specific solutions differ in the details, the overarching perspective is similar. The books propose a set of simplistic techniques, principles, and how-to's that are supposed to ease the difficulties of romantic human interaction and usually end up bending to the unfortunate stereotypes we all hear about regarding how men and women act in relationships. The *Complete Idiot's Guide to Dating* claims that it will teach you how to "get a date, have a great time, get a second date . . . turn friendship into love, and keep it hot." The *Mars . . . Venus* book has techniques for more modest goals such as how to motivate each other, avoid arguments, communicate, and ask for and get support. Not so bad, right? Yet it, of course, is based on the rather problematic premise that the book is necessary for survival because men are from Mars and women are from Venus — in other words, men and women have virtually no hope of understanding each other in relationships because it is as if they are from different planets. Lovely. We need not go into all of the thirty-five "rules" from *The Rules* that set out "practical," fifties-style guidelines for dating where women are basically supposed to sit at home, wait for phone calls, and then play hard-to-get once the phone rings.

The proposed solution to relationship hang-ups from all the books is pretty much the same. First, we must acquire an accurate understanding of human relationships, namely, that they are difficult and awkward human interactions that need to be navigated carefully to avoid hurting ourselves and others. Once this understanding is secure, we need to learn the techniques for manipulating the self and others toward whatever ends the individual or the couple chooses. Usually these "ends" have either to do with keeping the other person in our lives somehow or having great sex.

In technical, philosophical terms, the books propose a utilitarian "myth" about dating. Utilitarianism is an ethical theory that weighs actions purely based on their ability to achieve certain ends, with knowledge as a tool to improve one's technique. The utilitarian "myth" that these authors have created is the following:

Humans interact with other humans romantically, this interaction is fraught with peril, you must have the right techniques to avoid peril, and you need even better techniques to get pleasure out of the interaction.

The books bill themselves as providing the important but elusive techniques for the desired results: security and great sex.

Hence, the real problem here — the one that is really troubling despite the flippant titles — is that these books turn human beings into objects to be manipulated. They say you must do X, Y, and Z if you want to get A, B, and C from someone else. They are not guides on how to love others but on how to *control* others.

47

They make human relationships merely tactics for getting something from someone else. Love and friendship become words that sugarcoat the more brutal techniques of domination.

From a Christian and a spiritual perspective, the books have a very limited value. If you sift through the pages, you find many helpful tips, but you are also faced with a philosophy that undercuts our capacity to love others. Others are viewed as objects to be controlled instead of humans to befriend, love, and even find God hidden in.

The books are correct on one count though. They recognize the need to dispel many of the prominent but harmful dating myths. We do not doubt that there are plenty of harmful myths out there about dating. Otherwise we would not be writing this book in the first place.

We believe there is a better story to be told about dating — so here we are.

Popular Religion and Dating

Our cultural resources, while they did amuse us at times and offered glimpses of hope here and there, ultimately disappointed us on the topic of dating. Then we turned to popular Christian resources to see what we could find on the subject.

What we found there was almost as disappointing as our experiences with pop culture. Contemporary Christian authors seem to equate dating with sex, and in condemning sex condemn dating altogether. The problem gets worse: because dating is viewed with such intense suspicion, relationships in general are also looked upon with suspicion. Eventually, instead of love your neighbor, the mantra seems to become "fear your neighbor as they may lead you into sexual sin."

For obvious reasons, this disheartened us. In the following sections, we present an alternative to many popular Christian authors' view of dating and sex. We draw on many resources—cultural, theological, and spiritual, both ancient and contemporary — that we believe serve as a good foundation to understand dating in light of spirituality and Christianity today. The result is a full, rich, spiritual, and Christian understanding of the body, physical attraction, relationships, and dating.

One last note before beginning this section. What we criticize here is not Christianity itself, but rather particular authors' interpretations of Christianity. We firmly believe that Christianity has a lot to offer for relationships and love, and do not want these contributions lost simply because people mistake a particular Christian thinker as representing the whole Christian tradition.

We Can't Find the Word *Dating* in the Bible

OK, no matter what we do, where we look, and how hard we try, we can't find the word *dating* in the Bible. It just isn't there. The concept of *courtship* is there of course. That we already know. There is the story of Joseph's courtship with Mary and how he almost broke it off because he found out she was pregnant and he was not the father (Matthew 1:18–25). Jacob and Rachel's courtship lasted seven years. Jacob had to work for Rachel's father all that time so he could marry her (Genesis 29:1–28).

Love is present too. In the Song of Songs, erotic love is depicted in the relationship between a man and a woman. It is quite racy in fact; Christians and Jews alike have embraced this biblical text both as a description of ideal love and as a poetic metaphor about the love of God for humanity. (Bernard of Clairvaux, a twelfth-century mystic, and others dedicated entire spiritual texts to reflecting on this beautiful love poem.) There is also St. Paul's famous presentation of love in 1 Corinthians 13, where Paul describes the characteristics of love. It is patient, kind, not jealous, not pompous, not inflated, not rude, believes all things, hopes all things, endures all things, and never fails. It is the greatest of God's gifts. This is the reading we hear at weddings all the time.

Marriage is all over the place. There are the marriages of Abraham and Sarah, Isaac and Rebecca, and David and Bathsheba. Solomon had seven hundred wives (1 Kings 3). He was obviously a busy man. The prophet Hosea and many of the prophets after him used marriage as a metaphor of God's love for humanity. Although he himself does not marry, Jesus shows up at the wedding at Cana and turns water into wine to get the feast going (John 2:1–12).

There are examples of encounters with Jesus, where the two people meet, affect each other's lives, and then move on — similar to a dating relationship, just without the romantic part. There are people like Zacchaeus (Luke 19:1–10), Lazarus (John 12:1–2), the host of the Last Supper (Mark 14:13–15), Simon the leper (Mark 14:3), and Martha and Mary (Luke 10:38–42, John 11:1–45) who became involved with Jesus and his message after their encounter with him. They just didn't leave family, possessions, and livelihood behind. Instead, these people provided homes, food, and other resources to support Jesus and his fellow travelers.

Still, *dating* is not there.

What does this conspicuous absence of dating mean? Does it mean that dating as we typically define it — two people who meet, go out for a while in a romantic way and then break up — is simply prohibited within the context of Christianity? Does it mean that the Christian faith, spirituality, and dating simply aren't compatible?

We believe that just because we literally can't find the word *dating* in the Bible doesn't mean that dating relationships are out of bounds for Christians. It only means that literally the word *dating* isn't there. It also means that, as with all interpretation of texts, we need to open ourselves up to the text beyond the very words themselves. There is such depth in the Bible that to restrict ourselves to the literal words on its pages cuts us off from what the Bible can teach us in our world today, a world different from the ancient one.

Two thousand years separate our world from the lives and cultures of the people we read about in the Old and New Testaments. Today we have refrigerators, cable television, e-mail, chemotherapy, heart surgery, root canals, democracy, capitalism, communism, extreme sports, honeymoons in Las Vegas, and Elvis impersonators. We even have Krispy Kreme donuts.

The women's movement has brought about radical changes in the status of women over the past century. Women now seek bachelor's and master's degrees as well as Ph.D.'s, M.D.'s, and J.D.'s. In the best of circumstances, women choose their own professions, decide their own futures, and no longer need to depend on a husband to support themselves. Our mobility, along with our culture's emphasis on establishing a career before marriage, has led young people to postpone "settling down" into marriage for a decade or more to explore a chosen professional field, more study, traveling the world, or just the "freedoms" that a single life allows.

Marriage has simply changed. It is rare now that we marry following high school, and it is becoming rarer that we marry right after college. The twenty-something decade is turning out to be the age of singledom with young people often postponing marriage until their early thirties, if not even later.

Do these differences put our lives and practices outside the scope of biblical teachings? No, of course not.

The Bible gives us an understanding of the world, an understanding of how God's love for the world inspired God to save it. Those who believe in the story of Jesus see all of the good, bad, and oddness of the modern world in light of this love and are moved to act in accordance with this vision. Even though the Bible challenges our lifestyles today (as it did at the time it was written as well), this doesn't render the Bible irrelevant to our lives today nor does it necessarily mean that our modern lifestyle is sinful.

In other words, people can still eat donuts in a way that gives glory to God (which makes Jason very happy)! This may sound glib, but it is true to the degree that Christians are called to live their lives in light of the gospel. Living the same gospel story we find in this ancient text is possible even though donuts and dating are not explicitly found there.

So how do we go about figuring out an understanding of dating that is compatible with the Christian faith and spirituality? How *does* one apply the two-thousand-year-old message of a celibate, Jewish carpenter to our romantic interests?

Figuring this out is not easy. It requires, among other things, searching the Bible and mining its stories on the goodness of creation (Genesis 1), the fundamentally relational nature of human beings (Genesis 2), the love one can have for a stranger (Luke 10:29–37), the call to forgiveness (Matthew 6:14–15), and the love of God for humanity (John 3:16). It requires interpreting these stories to see dating as redemptive, helping us to experience not only better relationships with others, but also enhancing our closeness to God, even if dating turns out to be just a temporary encounter between two people.

If we allow the Bible to be the amazing book that it is, we'll discover that even two thousand years after Christ it can guide our lives, values, sense of self, and the ways — right and wrong — we interact with others. The Bible is God speaking to humanity. If we listen we'll hear what it has to say to us and our world today.

Why Some Christians Fear Dating

 Purity. Hell. Sin. Just a few little words strike fear into the hearts of Christians about dating. That's what motivates popular Christian writers like Joshua Harris to "kiss dating good-bye" and advocate that the rest of us should as well. We are told by the authors of books such as *Staying Pure, God's Design for Christian Dating,* and *Wait for Me: The Beauty of Sexual Purity* that the Christian teaching on dating can be summed up as follows: remain pure at all costs. These authors and others in this genre claim that protection of your purity before God is God's greatest desire for you, even if that means you must reject another's friendship and companionship, much less their love. They argue that if a friendship leads to attraction, attraction inevitably leads to lust, which inevitably leads to sex. Both lust and sex, of course, are sinful. So ending the friendship is the best way to protect oneself from sinning. They conclude that dating and sex go hand in hand. If you see someone that attracts you and are not yet ready for marriage, run the other way. Turn back from temptation before it is too late.

Save yourselves! Literally.

Sound familiar? If it does, then you've read books by authors like Joshua Harris and Rebecca St. James. You've come upon them in your search to understand the role of dating relationships in your faith life. You've read these authors because there is little else out there on the connection between spirituality, Christianity, and dating, and you want guidance on your desire to have loving relationships with others. You're familiar with the Bible, and you know too that both the word and the practice of dating are nowhere to be found in it. If you govern your life by the biblical teachings, you wonder whether it is OK to date at all.

And these books have encouraged you *not to date at all.*

If the above concerns don't sound familiar, then you may be someone who was raised Christian and then tuned out early. Once you started grappling with all of the difficulties of being a teenager and then a college student, you couldn't find much within Christianity to help you in your struggles with relationships and other challenges of life. Perhaps you even go to church every Sunday, but you tune religion out of the rest of your life because, unless you are celibate or married, there doesn't seem to be a place for you within the Christian faith. Or maybe your parents didn't bring you up within any tradition at all so until now religion has never been a serious concern for you. You date like most everybody else, or at least you hope to if somebody comes along who would like to date you.

But, perhaps leaving spirituality and religion completely out of your love life doesn't sit well. You are searching for something more meaningful in your relationships with others and find that losing your faith, or never really having it in the first place, has left you longing.

We believe there is hope.

Both of us disagree with the teaching that the best approach to dating is not to date at all. We believe (alongside many other Christians, both young and old) that the Christian faith does not require total abstention from dating. You do not have to stand outside of religion and spirituality until your lifestyle suddenly becomes "acceptable" when you get married.

To be fair, advocates of the anti-dating position take dating seriously and are concerned with the way it impacts our lives, for better or for worse. These authors are, at the very least, addressing a topic that many Christians seem afraid to even bring up in the first place. Anxiety about dating is not totally unwarranted. We all see how the media (sometimes accurately) portrays dating as an activity where individuals hop from person to person and often from bed to bed without commitment or concern for one another. In American culture, we experience a continuous depiction of infidelity, deception, exploitation, manipulation, promiscuity, violence, and abuse. Any human being should find these actions and images unacceptable, and question the medium and the minds they stem from. Given these circumstances, it's understandable that some suspicions about dating arise.

But again, though anti-dating advocates are willing to talk about dating, authors like Harris root their discussions in fear. This perpetuates an association of dating with the negative things like exploitation and promiscuity. Dating is then defined as the cause of pain and hurt to others and is reduced to sex.

Unfortunately both those who won't talk about dating and those who advocate no dating (or dating only when it will lead to marriage) have done dating a disservice. They both teach that dating and sex are synonymous. They equate dating with sex and immoral behavior. So, if dating and immorality are seen as one, then in rejecting sex, dating goes out the door too.

The rejection of dating, however, does not stop with sex. It extends even to friendship. Harris tells us that we should avoid male/female relationships, yet if we should somehow end up in one, we should end it quickly before we find ourselves liking the person more than "God would want us to." We (Donna and Jason) have been good friends for a long time and have never dated. We have both benefited greatly from our friendship. Yet, if we had taken the above advice we would have ended an extremely fulfilling and flourishing friendship. It doesn't seem to make sense that "God would want" us to turn away from each other because our friendship might lead to something more. What happened to loving our neighbor?

The *only* permissible way for a Christian to date, according to these books, apparently is when dating is "courtship," or when it will certainly lead to marriage. We see a major problem with dating only if and when it will lead to marriage. It seems then that the absolute best preparation for marriage, the best preparation for knowing how to relate to and love others, is to have as few relationships as possible, romantic or friendly. Again, save yourselves. Protect yourselves from others at all costs.

The best way to get ready for marriage is to have no prior relationships at all?

What?

With regard to the Christian faith and our spiritual lives, this particular approach to relationships worries us deeply. Practically speaking, we take issue with what this teaching says about how we are supposed to relate to others. Fearing dating and all it supposedly stands for implies a basic distrust of others. It promotes the idea that other people are out to hurt you in some way, to divert your attention from God, and/or to entice you to go against the Bible.

At its root, we believe this distrust is simply anti-Christian. Didn't Jesus call believers to love their neighbors? Jesus himself was always getting involved with strangers and outcasts, and they were the ones who often most fully embraced his message. As far as we know, he didn't say anything about only loving the neighbors you are not attracted to. The fact that God became a human being should persuade Christians to view every other person as if that person were God in disguise.

How are we supposed to learn to recognize God in others if we are taught to be afraid of them, or at least those who attract us in a special way? How are we to reconcile the teaching that we should turn away from others because they pull us away from what God wants for us with the teaching that it is through others that we can so vividly see God in this world?

It is true that dating sometimes goes wrong, very wrong. Sometimes it leads us to places we don't want to be with people who are not good for us. But dating is *not* inherently evil. Dating can be good. We have both had good relationships too. You have probably had good relationships too — relationships that included qualities like love, trust, mutual growth, and openness to others. These relationships help us to develop those qualities that make us better human beings and consequently better Christians.

We think dating can be done in an engaged, intelligent, and good way. We feel that spiritual growth is possible through loving others, even if they don't become our lifelong partner.

Of course, the difficult task we have ahead is explaining how intimately we are supposed to love our neighbors — but that is later. For now, let's put the fear, if indeed there is any, behind us.

Confusing Dating with Sex

When someone asked you out on a date, did you ever think that their question was really a veiled invitation for sex? OK, maybe the answer is yes if you are Sarah Jessica Parker's character on *Sex and the City.* For most of us, though, a date entails a coffee, maybe a little dinner, and, if it goes well, a kiss good night. But somehow our culture — and many Christian thinkers — just allow the imagination to run wild when it comes to dating.

When we talked to people about our project on dating, we had a number of wonderful conversations. People liked the topic and had lots of good ideas and stories of their own to share with us. We've heard everything from eighty-year-old married couples reminiscing about the times when they dated to young people from all walks of life who light up about the topic.

People have a lot to say about dating.

The only trouble we ran into was something neither of us expected. Some people were concerned that our project was really a legitimization of premarital sex. They couldn't seem to comprehend dating in any other way. This concern struck us as odd because our project, at least at that point in time, was more about the spiritual possibilities of dating than any overt concern about sex. It was very strange.

We weren't too worried about this confusion the first time it happened, but the third, fourth, and fifth time made us ponder what was going on. We worried even more as the mix-up came from smart and sincere individuals. How could they, much less anyone, confuse dating with sex?

That was our initial reaction. Then we started looking around for answers. We discovered that throughout our culture, dating *is* often portrayed as equivalent to sex. In newspapers, articles about teenage relationships focus on their sexual activity. We are bombarded by statistics about how often and at what age teenagers engage in sex. It's not as if the papers claim that dating and sex are *exactly* the same thing, but their focus on sex makes it seem as if it is the only significant part of dating relationships.

Newspapers are not alone either. As we said earlier, television and movies also often confuse sex and dating, but, like newspapers, do not always do it explicitly. The entertainment industry in general frequently uses sex to establish the seriousness of a relationship.

It is the sex that implies for the audience that two people are dating.

In the movie *Contact*, how do we know that the characters played by Jodie Foster and Matthew McConaughey like each other? They sleep together. On shows like *Buffy*, we learn that one character likes another often through their fantasies about sleeping together. How about on *Dawson's Creek?* The characters sleep together, but here it doesn't necessarily mean they like each other.

We aren't making a moral judgment about Hollywood or the media here. We are simply noting that our culture, like some Christian authors, often reduces dating to sex. Whether it is because of the ease of reporting statistics or the need to overtly signal the seriousness of a relationship, it leads many of us do the same.

So what is the Christian perspective on this subject, beyond the books on purity?

Just like popular culture, Christian theologians, and Catholic ones in particular, are inclined to equate dating and sex. The reasons, however, differ from the cultural ones.

Catholicism has been at odds with most of the modern world about the permissibility of sex and the resolution of its potential consequences. These "issues" are clearest in the Church's stance on contraception and abortion. The Catholic Church has stood out vocally, and many would say controversially, on these positions.

We do not want our discussion about dating to become a debate about abortion and contraception. The overpowering focus on these issues is the very thing we fought against during our initial conversations about spirituality and dating. Everyone seemed to want to turn the discussion about dating into a conversation about premarital sexuality and its consequences.

Instead, we would rather point out the implications of perspectives like the Catholic one that tends to immediately turn to sex and ultimately abortion in a discussion about dating. Basically the Catholic Church reduces almost all of its discussions of marriage, relationships, and dating to the issue of permissible and impermissible sexual intercourse in an effort to make a stand against premarital sex, contraception, and abortion. Any discussions having to do with relationships beyond friendship then automatically turn into discussions about sex, and when, where, and how it is OK and not OK.

From friendship to baby in a matter of seconds.

Even if a couple decides to get married, the Catholic Church focuses on the sex and issues around sex. Two friends of ours had an interesting story to tell regarding this issue. To get married in the Catholic Church, they had to go through a marriage preparation course, usually referred to as Pre-Cana. For many people Pre-Cana is a good experience. Questions of finances and values are brought to the foreground and discussed.

The experience of our two friends was different. They were frustrated by the whole course because it turned out to be a defense of natural family planning and an argument against contraception. It did nothing to address other practical issues about marriage. Our friends were left with the idea that the only significant issues in any relationship, married or not, were those pertaining to sex.

60

Regardless of what you think about contraception, this is bad marriage preparation, and involves a very narrow view of sex.

Why always this reduction of relationships to sex? Why all of this confusion?

The more we reduce dating and commitment to sex, and the more we reduce sex to the valid issues surrounding the consequences of sex, the more fear of dating becomes a reality if you are trying to be a Christian in today's world. And this fear spreads. It expands till it covers everything about romantic relationships, all the way from kissing to intercourse. Hence, we have Vincent Genovesi, the author of *In Pursuit of Love*, claiming that "deep (soul or 'French') kissing" is "unwise," "frustrative," and "dishonest,"[2] and Joshua Harris telling us why he "kissed dating good-bye" and why we should too.

So much for coffee, dinner, and a kiss good night if we are lucky. Apparently we are all expected to be a bunch of sex fiends, characters in a real-life *Sex and the City*, perhaps minus the cute, expensive shoes.

There may be a host of other reasons that contribute to the narrow focus. Dating is historically a new phenomenon so maybe the only way we can think about it is in terms of sex, because we do not know how else to define it. Human beings may just be more interested in sex than relationships. Certain Christian positions on sexual issues may be so controversial that everyone, both Christians and non-Christians, focus on them in lieu of anything else.

Regardless of the reasons, dating is not sex.

There are many dimensions to dating relationships, and the Christian tradition has many important things to say about love and relationships. But by equating dating with sex, the discussion is cut short and then dating is often dismissed altogether.

We are trying to open up the conversation a bit, to allow for some nuances. We will talk about dating. We will talk about sex.

We will talk about the two together. But we will be clear that they are not the same thing. The permissibility of dating and its compatibility with spirituality and Christianity are related yet not identical to arguments about sex and sexuality. We wish to give dating a fair hearing before we explore its implications for sexuality.

We will not confuse dating and sex.

Taking Spirituality Out on a Date?

We spent the last two sections exploring the ups and downs of pop culture and religion on the subject of dating. We have yet to say what we think dating is and how it is connected to spirituality. How can we take our spirituality out with us on a date?

We hinted at our discovery of the spiritual dimensions of dating in the first section with our personal stories, but in this section we take up the topic directly. Like all of our relationships, whether they are with friends or family, dating opens us to new people and new possibilities. Yet dating differs from these relationships in a very particular way.

In the following section, we discuss how the presence of eros distinguishes our dating lives and relationships. We use several different words to discuss eros and what its presence adds to our dating experiences on many levels. We call it a "spark" and say it focuses our feelings intensely on one individual. We say it is romance and that it causes people to be attentive to the needs and desires of another in creative and inspired ways. We even describe it as a falling in love and claim that it moves people to envision and enact new possibilities for themselves, their relationships, and even their larger communities. These aspects of eros combine to open us to new possibilities in our spiritual life and our relationship with God.

Before beginning this section, you should know that I (Jason) agree that we find God in and through relationships, yet believe that loving people and loving God, while inextricably linked, are not the same thing. I believe that loving God comes first because only then can we love people well, only then are we concerned about others' good and not just what makes them happy.

I (Donna) take a bit of a different perspective than Jason. In my own spiritual journey, I believe I have come to know and love God *through* loving others. It is in my experiences of human love that I am able to more vividly find and understand the divine. In loving others, I believe that I am loving God.

Enjoy.

Turning Toward Others

 Human beings need others. We need them to survive. Modern scientists talk about how babies cannot survive without parents to take care of them. This is unlike animals or fish that are able to walk or swim moments after they are born. Human beings also need others to be happy. Whenever we hear good news, we immediately want to share it with someone. Usually we seek out our best friend, but, if it is exceptionally good news, we usually tell the first hapless soul that wanders by us.

We need other people to know ourselves. After several years of living in Washington, D.C., I (Jason) thought I knew the place very well. I felt like I knew where things were and could get there. When I informed one of my friends how happy I was to be able to navigate a big city, however, he laughed at me and said, "You still have to ask directions to the movie theatre we always go to." His laugh made me realize that while it was true that I could get to where I wanted to go, I usually got lost on the way. Somehow I had blocked out this fact that was so obvious to my friends. They knew me better than I knew myself.

We need to turn toward others in order to live, grow, and prosper. This insight may not seem revolutionary, but, for many years, our culture has prized the individual. We believe that we must become "independent selves" in order to become responsible and mature adults. Famous developmental psychologists like Erik Erikson and Jean Piaget named this phenomenon "individuation." Feminist writers like Carol Gilligan and Jean Baker Miller have shown how this view of individuality and development often comes at the expense of healthy relationships. Their critique has spurred great interest in the central importance of relationships to human meaning, fulfillment, and mutual love. They conclude, and rightly so, that no matter what stage we are at in our lives, we are immersed in a network of relationships. Learning to be "ourselves in relation" is just as important as learning to be "ourselves as independent."

The beliefs of Christianity also deem relationships to be of the utmost importance. God is said to be triune, three persons in one nature, and thus fundamentally relational. God becomes human to relate to humans. Jesus gives two commands: love God and love our neighbor. Neither one of these can be fulfilled in total isolation. To be Christians, we must love, and hence be in some type of relationship, with God, self, neighbor, and enemy.

So relationships are important, but what do they do? What is their purpose in our lives?

Relationships in general are like openings to new worlds, invitations to love and to develop our capacity and understanding of love; they play a central part in our self-development. Viewing relationships in this manner implies that people must turn to each other for meaning and fulfillment in life. Since we contribute to each other's life journeys, relationships at a basic level are indispensable. Through relationships, we learn to view each other as potentially good and ultimately as occasions for encountering the divine in our experiences of the world.

This is how the two of us turned to each other in our own friendship. We have been close friends for a long time now, since graduate school. There weren't many young people in our program, so the younger generation of graduate students tended to gravitate toward each other. We also discovered we had some similar interests and a common friend, which led to hanging out away from school as well.

Our friendship evolved over the years and included many experiences (though we never dated each other). We have supported each other through countless difficulties. We have struggled through the trials and tribulations of a Ph.D. program by giving each other encouragement and advice. We have laughed a ton, gone to a lot of soccer games, played Play Station, ate lots of dinners and desserts together (we both really like chocolate), and have had more conversations about our respective love lives over the years than you could possibly imagine.

And, of course, those conversations gave rise to this book. We discovered a need for more resources on dating relationships. We wanted some help from religion and spirituality, but, ironically, our chosen academic fields and our religious tradition had little to say directly on the topic. So, we started working through what religion and spirituality might have to say to us about dating.

Ultimately we understand each other as gifts on our life journeys. We did not know what the gift was initially, but we trusted it to be something good. The result turned out to be an enduring relationship, one that not only provides us with support and love, but also pushes us to become better people and love others.

In addition to making us full and flourishing human beings, relationships also draw us closer to God. Our friendship has caused us to think, rethink, relate to, reflect on, pray about, and try to love God. We find these experiences to be at the root of the spirituality that grounds our friendship, a spirituality that has resulted from our agreements and disagreements and because of our unique backgrounds as well as mutual respect.   .

Dorothee Soelle, a feminist liberation theologian, captures the spirituality that emerged in our friendship and that can be present in any relationship. She not only focuses on how relationships are central to human life, but she also roots her understanding of spirituality and experience of God in those relationships. She wisely tells us in her many books on spirituality that relationships are the stuff that connects us most vividly to the divine. It is through the cultivation of all types of relationships that we become closer to God and that we become more loving people, better able to recognize the needs and concerns of others. In others, we are able to see and feel God operating in our lives, because it is through others that we can encounter love in all of its many dimensions and expressions. Relationships — whether they be with friends, family, spouses, or dates — provide us with some of the best experiences for developing our understanding of who God calls us to be, because they call us outside of ourselves toward the concerns and needs of another person and our larger community.

Throughout the Christian story, God is found in the face of the other. Jesus tells St. Paul to stop persecuting people because in doing so he is persecuting the Lord (Acts 9:4–6). Jesus tells his followers whatever people do to the others, they do to him (Matthew 25:40). Jesus is the Word that "dwells among us" (John 1:14). He even promises to be present when people come together (Matthew 18:20).

Thus, when we have relationships, when we turn toward others, we open ourselves up to new possibilities. We can grow and change as individuals, try new things, become better people, and even find God in and through our interactions. These possibilities are true of all relationships. The example we have used here is friendship, but we could have used a dating, marital, or familial example just as easily.

We will spend the rest of the book distinguishing dating from these other types of relationships, especially friendship and marriage. But, before we did that, we wanted to point out what dating shared with relationships in general. We wanted to note the possibilities that result whenever we turn to others.

When Friendship Isn't Enough

 We all know that friendship and dating are different (or at least they are supposed to be). We know, too, that one may lead to the other. We've also heard — from the movies, television, our friends, and maybe even ourselves — the line "I just want to be friends" used to end a relationship. We have watched Billy Crystal and Meg Ryan in *When Harry Met Sally* try that line and not be able to keep to it. There are even a few of us who have rushed into dating our friends, boldly claiming that "friendship simply isn't enough."

Yet, despite Harry and Sally's ultimate romantic success, many of us are apprehensive about dating that great man or woman you know who also happens to be a great friend. We are not sure if we want our friendship turning into romance.

We are afraid of losing the friendship.

Yet what exactly are the connections between dating and friendship? What are their differences? In "Turning toward Others," we talked about the similarities of dating and friendship. They are both relationships, and as such they both open us up to growing, trying new things, envisioning new ways of being in the world, and discovering God.

The major difference between dating and friendship is what the ancient Greeks called eros and what today we might call

68

the "spark" of a relationship, romance, falling in love, or physical attraction. Dating has this element to it; friendship does not. This is not to say that people who are friends are never physically attracted to each other — only that when the attraction is acknowledged, the relationship changes — it holds a new, romantic potential that may propel the relationship beyond friendship quite quickly.

Because of the romantic dimension that differentiates friendship from dating, the spiritual value of friendship and dating also differs. Friends enjoy the same subjects in school, play the same sport, watch the same movies, and read the same books. In his *Nicomachean Ethics*, Aristotle says that friends are mutually good for each other — friends make each other happy and friendship allows us the gratifying experience of sharing interests and values. Most importantly, friends share themselves but in a nonsexual way.

This platonic sharing is the spiritual value of friendship. Friends can love each other and enjoy each other's company even if they are not physically attracted to each other. Friendship sees value in people we may or may not find appealing to the senses. Friendship refuses to let us be limited by what can be seen by the naked eye. Thus, good friendships help us to look past superficial appearances and be open to the possibility of some good hidden beneath. For Christians, friendship is good because it helps believers to see past sickness, age differences, politics, race, gender, and creed in order to love others as God loves them.

Dating, however, has this "spark" which distinguishes it from friendship. Many claim that this element is just sexual desire and is thus problematic at best and evil at worst. But the "spark" is more than this. It draws us to a specific individual. We want to know more about and be with her or him. It binds people together in their concrete existence. Our love becomes very specific: it is directed toward the beloved in a very focused and intense way.

Far from being spiritually detrimental, this "spark" is the very value of dating. Dating actually starts to teach people ways to fulfill the demands of love. While in friendship, we learn not to limit our relationships to those with whom we feel a romantic spark; in dating we learn what it means for that romantic spark to inspire the relationship. Dating focuses our love and interest in another person in a way that is often deeper than friendship. While we have many friendships, we (at least most of us) only date one person at a time. In dating someone we try hard to learn what makes the person we date happy and sad. We learn what words move them and hurt them. And in finding out how to love one person inspired by that romantic spark, we have a head start on knowing what it means to love others in all our relationships — both future and current, including those without the romance. In dating, we receive a lesson in intimacy.

It is easy to see why many friends start to date: friends are sometimes attracted to each other. As friends, they already have some connection between them, spend time together, and care about each other. Add eros, and the two people can quickly move into dating.

The addition of eros, though, is why those who are concerned about dating ruining friendship have a genuine worry. The "spark" makes one individual attentive to another individual in a new way. Hence, the friendship is now transformed into a focus primarily on each other with an added physical dimension. Thus, it is much easier to move from friendship to dating, but not the other way around because adding the element of eros is much easier than removing it. Dating can build upon a friendship by just adding a physical element, but, in returning to just a friendship, the couple is cutting off this intense and focused love.

Sometimes it feels like a rejection. To successfully turn from dating back to friendship, both people not only need to understand the seriousness of the change but also be mature enough to live with it.

Thus, there are times when it is right *not* to date a friend. The two of us have been friends for a long time. We have a common intellectual curiosity, connect on a philosophical level, and share experiences about teaching and relationships. Even our differences do nothing but deepen and strengthen what binds us together.

Yet we have never dated. Why?

We have never had that "spark" between us.

Still, given that we share so much and spend a lot of time together, shouldn't we risk a romantic relationship? Probably not. Not that it would be wrong to date, only that for us, the friendship is too strong while the prospect for successful dating without the "spark" is too weak. By dating, we would be jeopardizing something wonderful for something we doubt would work out. Given the strength of our friendship, we would have to be pretty sure about our romantic compatibility for us to risk it. Luckily we have been fortunate to understand the relationship and what we see as its natural boundaries with regard to romance, thus preserving our friendship. And by respecting those boundaries, we have the benefit of enjoying the specialness that friendship has offered us over the years.

Some of our friends are not as lucky. When we asked our friend Kelly about dating a friend, she said, "Do not date friends out of boredom!" When we asked her to explain, she said that just because there are no other options does not mean that you should risk dating your friends. "You should only date a friend," she went on, "because you are attracted to the person in a way that goes beyond friendship." In other words, do not endanger the friendship if you have no good reason to do so.

Does this mean that we should *never* risk a friendship for a romantic relationship?

We think never taking the risk goes too far. Friendships are based on common virtues, experiences, and interests as well as affection. There is no doubt that a person you share these commonalities with can be a good person to date given the right level of confidence about it working out. In fact, dating often flourishes when it stems from a friendship.

We talked about why the two of us (Jason and Donna) do not date, but I (Donna) am now in a romantic relationship that grew out of a friendship — a *really close* friendship.

I met Josh about eight years ago because he was dating one of my best friends, Heather. Though Josh and Heather broke up shortly after I met him, Josh and I stayed in touch and quickly grew to be close friends. Over the many years of our friendship, we shared the ups and downs of life, visited each other, ran a marathon together, laughed a lot, talked of things both silly and profound, but dating was never a possibility that we formally put on the table. There were a couple of good reasons for this. One was that I did not want to hurt Heather. Another was that whenever Josh was single, I was dating someone and vice versa. We never seemed to be single at the same time. It seemed easier that way anyhow. We didn't have to deal with the messiness of facing our potential as a couple — or the potential effect it might have on our friendship.

Well, Heather got married. She found the man of her dreams. One issue was resolved. Then Josh and his long-term girlfriend broke up, and shortly after that, the relationship that I was in ended as well.

Then we saw each other one night, after not having seen each other since Heather's wedding. Sparks flew.

Despite sparks flying, birds chirping, and all the traditional signs that love was in the air, Josh and I did not jump into dating.

We sat with the sparks for a while in our own respective corners. When we finally got up the guts to tell each other what we were feeling, we were really excited but also nervous. We didn't want to jeopardize such a long-term and special friendship. In the end our feelings were too powerful *not* to date. (By the way, when I nervously told Heather that Josh and I were going to date, her wonderful response was, "What took you so long?")

Dating for Josh and me turned out to be a good idea, and our friendship has served as a strong foundation on which to build a relationship. When you date a friend, mutual respect, care, trust, and a shared history are already present between you. These are important qualities that often take a good deal of time to establish if you choose to date someone you've just met. With friends, you start a dating relationship at a different level, which is nice. Also, in terms of developing a spiritual dimension to the relationship, which requires a certain level of trust, connection, and effort, past friendship provides a good foundation on which to explore the possibilities.

But dating a friend is always a risk. Luckily Josh and I are still together.

And, so are Jason and I.

Thus there are times when friends should not date: when there is no romantic chemistry in the friendship, when the friendship is extremely valuable and the possibilities of successful romance are slim, or when you are just bored and feeling kind of lonely. Yet there are also times when friendship is not enough, and the risks are worth taking.

Opening Up to Romance

 Once during a class on marriage, some of the students ended up in a discussion about the loss of romance in relationships. From various corners of the room came shouts such as: "After the first few months, everything becomes boring." "He danced with me when we first went out. Now he won't. He says he only did it so I would go out with him in the first place." "In the midst of work and children, there is not any time for romance." "I miss romance. All we ever do now is sit around and watch TV."

Then a voice from the back of the room chimed in: "My husband left me a stuffed bear and chocolates this past Valentine's Day."

The classed paused because this nontraditional student had been married for over twenty years. How could this woman have romance in such a long-standing relationship? It was as if this woman had said she was able to fly. The class sheepishly admitted their admiration for such an act of love, and the woman blushed with the praise of the class.

Many of us stand in awe of this woman's marriage. Why is romance so scarce in a world that seeks it? Is it genuinely special? Is it a sign of a good relationship? Or is romance just some cultural fabrication used to make us buy new products?

We started reading books to find out what was said about romance and came across an article entitled "Beyond Romance to Human Love" in *Perspectives on Marriage*.[3] The author, Robert Johnson, began by saying that authentic love is a recognition and appreciation of another person. Love pulls people out of their own ego and into the larger world. So far, we were all in agreement.

Johnson, however, continued by claiming that authentic love was the *opposite* of romance. He said that romantic love arose only when people first meet. Since people do not know each other well

74

at the very beginning of a relationship, there is no way for them to appreciate each other. Thus, those first romantic impulses are merely a projection of one person's desires onto the other person. Romantic love is selfish and the opposite of true love.

We were *not* in agreement with this assertion.

We were surprised by his claim, and disappointed. Sure, we all know people who "are in love with love." We know people who are in relationships just for the sake of being in them. Yet how can one claim that *all* romantic love is self-centered?

The husband who gave his wife a teddy bear and chocolates on Valentine's Day did not seem to be acting in a self-centered way. He appeared attentive to his wife's happiness and so was acting romantically. Somehow he knew that leaving a sweet gift for her would contribute to her happiness and communicate his feelings of love for her in a way other than just saying it in words — hardly a negative act.

The other students' complaints — he doesn't dance anymore, we only watch television, and so on — stem from a lack of attention to or appreciation of each other. The disappointment in these statements also implies that at one point in the relationship the two people were open to each other's wants and desires. At one point, they *did* dance. Acts of romance seem to come from genuine concern for each other, not selfish wishes as Johnson claimed.

Somehow romance seems an essential dimension that distinguishes a dating relationship from just an ordinary one, contributing to whether or not we experience the relationship as good and how we express that goodness to each other. So how, then, does romance add to our spiritual lives?

When Julie and Adam met and began dating, every single time they went out, Adam showed up for the date with a present for Julie. Sometimes it was flowers. Sometimes it was chocolates. He opened doors and all of that. Her friends, many of them strong feminists, were critical of his approach to the relationship claiming that his efforts were sexist. But Julie did sweet things for him too. The gestures were not expressions of superiority or inferiority but of mutual attraction. The actions were one way they expressed themselves in the relationship.

These gestures are a part of the *language* of dating, a wonderful part.

When two people meet, realize that they are attracted to each other, and decide to go on a date, romance like that between Adam and Julie often flourishes. This kind of romance doesn't just happen in relationships today either. The Song of Songs is a beautiful example of romantic love moving two people to appreciate each other. The man speaks of the woman's eyes like "doves," lips like "scarlet strands," and a neck like "David's tower." He concludes by claiming she is "all-beautiful, my beloved, and there is no blemish in you" (4:1–7). The woman does her share of praise as well saying the man has arms like "rods of gold," a body as "a work of ivory," and a stature like "the trees of Lebanon" (5:9–15). She ends with the proclamation that "he is all delight" (5:16).

Because the Song of Songs is found in the Bible, the poem affirms not just romantic love but the possibility that such a love can be linked to God's love for humanity. Judaism and Christianity have both elaborated on this connection. The former traditionally reads the poem as a metaphor for God's love of Israel and the latter as a metaphor for Christ's love of the Church. These additional layers of interpretation imply that as people learn to appreciate each other, they may progress from the experience of loving each other to the desire to love more than just each other. They may move from love within this primary relationship to love of all humanity and an appreciation and love for the world. This progression may ultimately lead to the experience of the root of all love that, as we learn from the Song of Songs, is found in God.

In a sense, Judaism and Christianity view romantic love not just as an appreciation between lovers but as a means of appreciating God. Our romantic love of each other is analogous to God's love for humanity. Hence, romance is a way to love each other but also can become a way to love God. This is not a replacing of romantic love with a love for God, but finding God in and through these romantic feelings.

This is why the Song of Songs is important in our discussion about dating. It recognizes that all kinds of love open people up to each other and ultimately open them to God. It is a beautiful, ancient, and biblical example of two people longing for each other, taking delight in each other, and engaging in this wonderful process of "romancing" that not only makes them happy but also helps them experience God's love as present within the world.

And, for romance to happen, we need people to express the way they feel toward the person they date — like Adam did in bringing Julie flowers, like Julie did through her sweet acts.

Romance is good because through it we make each other happy, we make each other blush, we make each other's hearts flutter. We do nice things to show we like another person. We are concerned about them and appreciate them. We are attracted to them in a special way. When we act romantically, we consider what someone else would like and make the effort to go about actualizing it. Far from being egocentric, romance seems to be about our attentiveness outward toward another person, about loving people in their concreteness. It has to do with opening up.

Romance doesn't have to be grandiose either. Sure, surprise bouquets of flowers and fancy dinners are nice. But romance also includes simple acts — attentive listening, a walk on a nice evening, remembering important dates. We find romance in many forms, but its constant element seems to be an openness to the needs and wants of others.

Romance is a language we learn by dating. The only way to become proficient in the language of romance is for us to practice it with each other.

We realize, of course, that the moments of romance alone do not make love. We know that romantic gestures can also be false, manipulative, and intended to make one person indebted to another, what Johnson correctly identifies as selfish acts. Flowers alone can not save a date between two people who are just not right for each other or a long-term relationship that needs to end.

We agree with Johnson that love recognizes and appreciates the other. We would add that love in a relationship needs to be mutual and expressed by more than an occasional dinner. The fullness of love is more than romantic love, but it does include it. Romance should not be the opposite of love. The fullness of love requires that the opening made by romance become a permanent doorway. That romantic moment of appreciation needs to be expanded until it becomes not just an occasional act but a habit. According to Aristotle, habits bring some potential we have to its fulfillment through repeated action. Hence, we "become builders by building houses, and harpists by playing the harp. Similarly, we become just by the practice of just actions, self-controlled by exercising self-control, and courageous by performing acts of courage."[4] We extend Aristotle's insight by saying that the fullness of love results from the repetition of romantic acts of love. We come to true love by practicing love.

One last thing.

Romantic love involves a moment when one person demonstrates awareness of another. It is attentiveness to what makes another happy. Yet these peak moments are only moments, and, on a first date, they may signify little more than a wish to get to know someone, an attraction to a person, or an excitement about him or her. Romantic love is an opening of one person to the other. It is not love in its fullness. The fullness of love demands more. Yet love needs this opening in order to grow.

Romance calls us to go through the opening and live on the other side.

Falling in Love Is a Spiritual Shift

 At the beginning of the book, I (Donna) talked about how, in a conversation over dinner with my friend Gene, I found in myself an intense yearning for a spiritual dimension in relationships, especially my romantic ones. I wanted dating to be more meaningful and realized my desire to set my romantic relationships in the context of a larger spiritual path.

I knew something was shifting in me with regard to spirituality and relationships, but I wasn't sure how to articulate it. It felt good and exciting. Yet everything that is good and exciting is not always easy (of course). Because of my long-term discomfort with religion (and Christianity in particular), opening up spiritually was difficult and strange, but I knew I had to do it. I knew it was important.

After some reflection and lots of talks with Jason, I realized that this shifting was not as strange as I had thought. I had felt these new feelings and desires before, but hadn't linked them to spirituality.

Many scholars and authors who write on the topic of spirituality, in addition to talking about spiritual journeys and the possibilities of spiritual growth in our lives, also talk about a "shifting" that happens to us as we travel down a spiritual path. Sometimes it occurs at the beginning of the way — it is what causes the spiritual journey to be taken up. This is what happened to Zacchaeus when he met Jesus. He immediately gave half his possessions to the poor, and anyone he had defrauded, he repaid four times over (Luke 19:1–10).

But this shifting doesn't always happen as suddenly as it did for Zacchaeus. Sometimes the shifting is the stuff of the journey itself. Peter had faith in Jesus, so he walked on water but then became afraid and sank (Matthew 14:22–33). He proclaimed Jesus to be the messiah but then thought that the messiah must not suffer and die (Mark 8:27–33). Finally, he insisted that he would never betray Jesus (Matthew 26:35) only to betray him three times (Matthew 26:69–75). Peter's continual shifting is the journey that ultimately leads him to be the "rock" of the church (Matthew 16:18).

Bernard Lonergan is a theologian who talks about the role of shifting views, or "horizon shifts," and how these shifts come about. For Lonergan, one of the most vivid horizon shifts occurs when we fall in love with someone. He discusses how, when we fall in love, all of our spontaneous interests and desires are reoriented in light of our new love. Falling in love is an experience where we suddenly see the world in a whole new and beautiful way. Our experience of the object of our love can awaken us to the world anew.

While I (Donna) struggle to relate to a spiritual journey like that of Peter, falling in love I can understand. Many of us have experienced that "birds are chirping, everything is blooming, oh what a happy day" feeling after staying up late and talking for hours with someone we think is wonderful and amazing. This experience makes us feel as if we are on top of the world and that anything is possible. Shakespeare compared his beloved to a "summer's day" (Sonnet 18), said she caused him to sing "hymns at heaven's gate" (Sonnet 29), and found "not marble nor the gilded monuments" able to outshine her (Sonnet 55).

Falling in love tends to move us to radically new ways of feeling, acting, and thinking. It opens us to new possibilities of being who we are by showing us who we can be with another.

A good example we have for this phenomenon is our friend Todd. Before he fell in love, he liked video games, cartoons, and soccer — standard adolescent interests. When he met Angel, he suddenly began to like different things. He became interested in tae kwon do, vacationing, and being financially responsible. He changed. Financially responsible? This was not Todd.

And yet it was. Angel had not forced him into any of this. He grew into them naturally and freely just as his affections for her had. He was becoming more *than* what he was, maybe even more of *who* he was. He discovered new interests and desires and was extremely happy. This was falling in love — his horizon shifted and his understanding of the world expanded.

New possibilities for self-understanding sometimes come from the embrace of someone else or from an opening up and merging another's perspective with one's own. People who fall in love open each other up to new ways of being in the world — they cause each other to shift.

We believe that our experiences of falling in love as we date deepen our understanding of the love of God in our lives. As falling in love with someone causes us to see the world in a new light, so a sense of God's love in our *love* lives can help us to see our romantic relationships in a new light and with new meaning as well. If at the root of our relationships with God is a call to love, then the practice of love in our dating lives is one way in which we respond to a divine call or our desire to experience meaning in a more ultimate way.

Unfortunately, falling in love is often derided as a superficial experience. We hear people say that falling in love is not real love. Real love only appears after these initial, giddy feelings have faded. This would probably be the position of Robert Johnson whom we cited earlier. Johnson described romantic feelings as purely self-centered and ultimately not about love at all, so understanding our experiences of falling in love in a spiritual light would probably be out of the question for him.

We don't deny that relationships and love need to go deeper than that of initial attraction, but we do maintain that falling in love is a type of love — one that is similar to and can open us up to how spirituality and dating go together. The experience of falling in love — even when that love turns out to be temporary — is important for understanding one's relationship to others, the world, and God. When we fall in love, we experience concretely what it means for our world to suddenly change through the introduction of someone significant in our life. This experience helps us to understand what it means to live a spiritual life: living in such a way that God's love or our pursuit of ultimate meaning transforms how we experience the world and relationships. Falling in love opens us to the possibility of a deeper understanding of this type of transformation. It is an avenue in life that vividly teaches us to understand what a spiritual horizon shift is all about.

Lonergan said that once love "has blossomed forth and as long as it lasts it takes over. It is the first principle. From it flow one's desires and fears, one's joys and sorrows, one's discernment of values, one's decisions and deeds."[5] When we fall in love it is as if someone gives us new glasses that alter our vision. It makes us see the world as full of possibility. New experiences are viewed with excitement and openness. We begin to trust. Falling in love opens us to a new person. This new person appears to us as someone who can bring new experiences to us, inspire us to grow, and expand our way of thinking.

Falling in love is one way we express ourselves as being made in God's image. Dorothee Soelle, a Protestant theologian and writer on spirituality, calls all of us "to become lovers like God is a lover." And how does God love? God sees the world as good (e.g., the creation story in Genesis) and even pursues us like a being in love (e.g., the book of Hosea).

Falling in love makes people appear to us as gifts (not as a threat or temptation, like many Christian authors would lead us to believe).

We are thus called to love like this: seeing people as good, as gifts, and as potentially opening us to God and to new spiritual horizons. And falling in love, which Lonergan says "plucks out the heart of stone . . . [and] implants a heart of flesh," makes this possible. It radically moves us to a new way of viewing the world such that what once was threatening now is joyful. Falling in love opens us to someone new *and* causes us to experience the divine gift that others are to us. It causes us to trust in the world a bit more. If we open ourselves to falling in love, then we are more ready to accept the divine presence that comes hidden in others, a presence that, perhaps, we have also hidden from ourselves. We become more open to God and the world, and consequently, all things become possible.

Dating Opens Our Eyes

We spent the last section talking about what dating is and how its particular dimensions uniquely lead us to spiritual growth and love of God. In this section, we draw out these dimensions even further. We say that dating can open us to the deeper realities of life and faith in a way different than relationships with our friends, acquaintances, and family. We explore how dating may be viewed as part of a greater journey, what we call a "clue" to a mystery. In viewing dating this way, we believe that it can strengthen our spiritual life—dating becomes a place where we experience God's love in the world.

One last thing: though we discuss in this section how eros is communicated in various ways through our dating experiences, we do not yet explore one of its most common expressions: sex and sexuality. Sex and sexuality in dating will be the main focus of the section that follows this one.

You will have to hang on to those questions a bit longer.

Making Dating Meaningful

A lot of people in college and their twenty-something years develop an interesting habit. Every weekend turns into a search to find the new "significant other of the moment," not Mr. or Mrs. Right, but Mr. or Mrs. Right Now. Each Friday night is a quest at parties or at bars to find someone new to make life interesting for the evening. The culture is such that the one evening often turns into nothing more. Literally *nothing* more. Not even a phone call. Sometimes not even a last name. On Sunday mornings, the Friday or Saturday night "date" — if you can even call it a date — turns quickly into a memory and often a memory that feels empty. Lonely. Until of course another Friday night opens up a whole new host of opportunities. It seems that a lot of people try to affirm the cultural and religious expectations surrounding dating that we've talked about: that dating is really a veiled forum for casual sex.

What we discuss above as typical to the lives of many, single young people is a far cry from the previous essay where we describe dating as a potential occasion for spiritual transformation, love, and a deepening of our relationship with God. The type of dating depicted here is both emotionally exhausting and a spiritually empty cycle, not to mention an invitation for all of the problematic consequences of casual sex including unplanned pregnancy and sexually transmitted diseases.

Yet how many of us have gone on date after date without even a thought? How many of us have jumped from relationship to relationship or night to night as if we were jumping from stone to stone at the beach, our eyes fixedly on the next one, securing our footing and then quickly moving on?

It is this type of "dating" that Christian authors, youth ministers, and parents alike are worried about. Their worries are not unjustified. Though this type of dating may seem fun and exciting when we first engage in it, ultimately we find it involves a self-destructive and potentially dangerous pattern of behavior, a pattern that will not lead quickly to discovery of the spiritual dimensions of our dating relationships.

The flip side of this activity is that some people come to observe dating as a frenetic and frustrating game, often self-emptying, destructive, and emotionally exhausting. They dislike what dating has become for many, particularly during college, and decide not to give dating a chance. Or they don't date because they worry that there are no other types of relationships than what our pop and reality-obsessed culture equates with dating. If they are Christian, they may hear Joshua Harris's warnings and agree that dating only leads to un-Christian behavior, so why date at all?

The above conceptions about dating are limiting to say the least: either engage in damaging behavior or stay away from dating altogether. Only a small minority finds another, healthier path, and sometimes only after years of destructive, emotionally exhausting experiences in dating.

Yet dating does not have to be this way for any of us.

Dating does not have to be a series of haphazard leaps from one date to the next or from one person to another. It does not have to be a succession of random hookups that leave us feeling empty and alone in the morning. Nor does healthy, Christian behavior require us to say "no" to dating altogether. We can engage in dating without the loss of our integrity or spirituality. Dating can be meaningful, spiritually significant, and transformative.

As scholars in the area of religion, we often hear St. Anselm's pronouncement that defines theology as "faith seeking understanding." This phrase has broader implications. It calls us to reflect on what we have, are, and do. It calls us to move from simply undergoing our experiences to reflecting, contemplating, and analyzing our experiences. As we do this, "a circle of evaluation" is created. Reflecting on our religious experience, ritual, symbol, and tradition produces insights about these experiences that in turn (ideally) deepens our experience of religion, faith, and spirituality in the future. And the process continues over again. A dialogue of faith and understanding, of experience and reflection occurs. It is a reciprocal relationship — a "coupling" of two things that make a more meaningful and insightful whole, expanding our relationship with God and deepening our spiritual lives.

It is this same coupling of our experiences with reflection that opens us to the spiritual dimension of dating relationships. We believe that the joining of our experiences in relationship with reflection on those experiences is an essential element bringing our dating lives and spiritual lives together.

Unlocking these possibilities begins with simply asking questions, a simple communication with oneself and with the other person. Why are we dating? How does dating affect us, our friends, our family, those we are dating, those we have dated? What does dating someone inspire in us? How does dating affect our understanding of the good, the true, the real, and the beautiful? How does it impact our prayer life?

If you are a Christian, you might wonder how dating fits in with what God wants for you and your partner. If you are not Christian, you may wonder how spirituality fits in with your interest in dating and whether or not your partner is interested in spirituality at all. Simultaneously you may also be struggling to define what spirituality means for you.

We need not date at the frenetic pace of the rest of our lives today, particularly when we're in college. Though pausing to ask questions and reflect on the spiritual dimensions of dating may sound simple, stopping the hectic pace of life in college and post-college is often harder than we might imagine. Our lives today don't offer much space for contemplation. We go, go, go, and do, do, do — and our dating reflects this same pattern if we are not intentional about it.

Contemplation and communication open up new worlds and possibilities for us in our relationships. We start to reflect about where our experiences are taking us and how our past affects us. We reflect on our own integrity and the integrity of others. Our questions move us to ask deeper questions of ultimate meaning; why are we here and what is the meaning of life? We begin to see dating in light of these concerns. In pursuing these reflections, dating becomes meaningful in new ways — it offers us a place in our lives for a deeper experience of the world and relationships — where we discover the meaning that a special kind of intimacy with another person can bring to us.

Still the process of reflection is not easy. Meaningful dating requires patience and effort, two aspects of life with which people struggle. We have become used to constant activity and instant gratification.

In the Benedictine monastic tradition of Christian spirituality, there is a process called *lectio divina*. *Lectio divina* involves a kind of contemplative prayer that occurs as someone reads aloud from a religious text, often an excerpt from the Bible. The listeners seek to open themselves to the words in a way that they might be transformed by those words as they listen. They are to "chew" on the words slowly, as if enjoying an incredible meal, so that they might experience the full flavor and possibility of their meaning, opening themselves to the divinity embedded in the text.

Benedictine monks and nuns engage in *lectio divina* every day, because they believe it is a process that opens them to God's presence in their lives. This daily experience of listening to sacred words helps one become especially attuned to the voice of God. It's that coupling of experience and reflection again.

For dating to become meaningful, it must follow a similar (though not identical) process. Benedictines engage a text to find the presence and encounter the depths of God — hoping to be transformed through the intimacy experienced through this type of relating. In dating, we engage others for a similar higher purpose — to discover the depths of another person and the depths of the love and mutual transformation possible through this intimacy. A monks reflects on the words, stays with them at length, listens to their meaning, opening to growth in their relationship with God. In dating we reflect on another person, we "stay" with them in a focused way, if only temporarily, we "listen" to their meaning, opening ourselves to growth and transformation through the experience of this other person. This reflecting, staying, listening, and opening of ourselves to another, is central to the spiritual dimensions of dating.

By seeking to understand the significance of our experiences in relationship, we may find ourselves already on a spiritual journey — if we allow ourselves to call it that. And from this understanding, dating already means more.

Getting a "Clue" about Dating

What exactly is dating about? People often claim that dating is merely preparation for marriage. Others believe it is just a recreational activity. Perhaps you have some other understanding of dating. We have struggled to figure out the meaning of dating. Our dating in high school and college did not seem much like courtship. We took our relationships seriously but did not feel that they would lead to marriage. Not that we were opposed to marriage either. It's just that marriage was not really on our radar then. During high school, we were figuring out who we were, who other people were in relation to us, and what we wanted to do with our lives. Marriage, while a possibility, seemed both remote and irrelevant. Who to go to the prom with was a much more pressing concern.

Still, in high school we weren't just dating for recreational purposes. We recognized that the people we went out with were *people*. Even if we just went out on one date, we did not want to hurt or use our date. While dating was enjoyable (most of the time), the pleasure of it did not seem to be the only reason why we went out.

So what do we mean when we use the term *dating*? Can we somehow come up with a definition of dating? Do we need to define dating differently depending on our respective time in life — high school, college, post-college? Or can we find a generic definition that fits with every age and persuasion?

We decided that coming up with one definition for dating today would not work — it is difficult to define something that can mean so many different things depending on the context. Yet when the two of us got together to discuss our own dating experiences for the purposes of this book, we realized we needed to figure out a clearer understanding of what we meant when using the term *dating*. We thought that you, the reader, might want to know what we understand dating to be and to involve, even if we do not come up with a very specific definition.

So, we ended up coming up with two metaphors to help understand what we think the concept of dating is about: a clue that helps one solve a mystery or provide assistance on a journey.

We got to this conclusion in a roundabout way. The two of us had talked about our personal experiences, but we needed some perspective a little more distant from ourselves. So, we turned to books and movies about people in relationships.

We talked about Jane Austen's *Pride and Prejudice*. In the story, Elizabeth is an intelligent, quick-witted, good person who does not bend to the social pressures to marry for security or social status. Her only fault is that she occasionally judges people too quickly. She meets Mr. Darcy, a wealthy bachelor who is also intelligent and good but views himself as superior to almost everyone. The two eventually come together and fall in love, but only after Elizabeth's prejudice toward Darcy has been undone and Darcy's pride has been eliminated.

We also discussed Philip Pullman's *His Dark Materials* fantasy trilogy. (We are both fantasy geeks.) At the end of the story, Lyra (the heroine) finds herself in predicaments she did not choose. She must decide between staying with Will, her first love, and accomplishing a larger good that would affect the world. She freely (and painfully) decides for the good of the world. When Will and Lyra each return home and close all of the windows between them, they are both transformed. Both have loved, sacrificed, and become wise because of their adventure, but ultimately do not end up together.

We thought about the films *Shakespeare in Love* and *Ten Things I Hate about You* as well. In the first, Shakespeare has writer's block and Viola de Lassep seeks poetry in her life. When they finally get together, Shakespeare overcomes his difficulties and Viola experiences poetry. Unfortunately they must part, but they are significantly different as a result of their time together. In *Ten Things I Hate about You* (based on Shakespeare's *Taming of the Shrew*), Patrick Verona is viewed as a volatile rebel and Kat Stratford is hostile to everyone. Through the various circumstances that bring them together, Kat's view of the world becomes more open and Patrick's goodness emerges.

Finally, we read Dorothy Day's autobiography, *The Long Loneliness*. Dorothy Day is a twentieth century spiritual figure who is famous for starting the Catholic Worker movement, which supports homes that shelter and feed those in need all across the United States. In her autobiography, Day explains how she learns to love creation and sees its beauty through her longtime lover Forster. Yet, in loving creation she discovered her love of God, which brings her into conflict with her partner. Day's encounter with Forster changed the way she viewed the world, but, in the act of changing, the relationship no longer became viable. Day felt she had to leave in order to continue her journey toward God.

How might these stories help us to understand dating?

We noticed that these stories all had a similar structure. The main characters were trying to be faithful to what they believe (Elizabeth/Darcy and Kat/Pat), searching for a solution to their problems (Lyra/Will and Shakespeare/Viola), or trying to discover meaning in their life (Day/Forster). When the two characters came together, they ended up helping each other with their faithfulness, problem, or search. Finally, the relationship didn't always last forever even though both people greatly benefited from it.

We reflected on this pattern. In all of these stories, we learn that everyone has a higher purpose, a larger journey, or something important to learn, which they discovered through their experience of the relationship. The characters are searching for life's meaning, a heightened sense of self and direction, or something that is central to the happiness of the couple themselves and often others as well. Fulfilling this higher calling to us seems like a journey or quest to be completed or a mystery to be solved. The relationship between the two people is not the journey or mystery itself. Instead, the relationship, or what we loosely think of as dating, is an integral part of fulfilling the journey or discovering aspects of the mystery.

This insight was the "clue" for us. We started to think of dating as a clue to a mystery. This metaphor helped us understand why dating can be significant. A clue is something concrete — some bit of clothing, a note, or overheard words — that contributes to solving the mystery. Dating also works through something concrete — what we have called at times a spark, romance, falling in love, and physical attraction — to arrive at a deeper understanding of the meaning and purpose of life, one's relationship with others, and one's relationship to God. Dating helps reveal our personal journey through our concrete experiences of the relationship. Ultimately, the relationship should help both people become better humans and better Christians.

But couldn't friendship and marriage also be thought of as "a clue"? Perhaps, but if we are using the metaphor of clue and mystery, friendship and marriage fit better with different understandings. We have talked about friendship as platonic. This interest in each other does not stem from romance or falling in love. Thus, while it contributes to understanding the "mystery" of life, it does not have that physical dimension. A friend is like the wise bartender who an investigator goes to when she is stuck on a case, the butler who knows as much as the master, or the person who has the gadgets to help the heroine. A friend is that go-to person that we need for advice, support, and, sometimes, just some information.

Marriage, too, is different. It does have the physical dimension to the relationship and contributes to one's understanding of the world and relationship with God. Yet marriage is more than a clue. Spouses are the individuals with whom one solves the case, or at least where we embark on a new and different mystery.

Thus, we believe our definition of dating as a clue is helpful (even if it is somewhat odd) because it contributes to our understanding of ourselves as persons, as parts of a community, and as creatures in relationship with God. Dating helps us on what we have been calling life's mystery or journey. We use these terms not just metaphorically but also because mystery and journey are both used to describe aspects of the spiritual life. Rudolf Otto, a twentieth century philosopher of religious experience, uses the term *mysterious* in describing our experiences of God, and journey is a central metaphor for the Christian mystics when articulating the development of their intense relationships with the divine. Dating relationships (when we do not reduce them to sex) can be rich occasions for experiences of God and our relationship to the divine. These experiences not only bring us closer to each other, help us gain our sense of self, and understand our purpose in life, but they also contribute to our spiritual identities, development, and relationship with God.

And, at the foundation of these experiences of dating, though at different levels and degrees, is love. Dating helps us to understand that we are relational creatures and that through relationships we learn what it means to love another person in a one-on-one relationship. While we can learn about loving through friendship, in dating we learn about love and intimacy through romance, falling in love, and physical attraction. This difference, we believe, is significant for having a loving, intimate relationship with God. In *To Work and to Love: A Theology of Creation*, Dorothee Soelle talks about the love between a couple as ideally spilling over into the larger community. She sees this type of one-on-one loving, both marital and non-marital, as an integral part of a Christian community and spiritual growth.

Understanding dating in this manner means that it is part of the larger picture of spirituality. We know that's a pretty lofty view. After all, dating often begins with a smile at someone we think is attractive, or with some coffee after class. But it is in these physical interactions that the possibilities of love, romance, intimacy with another person and intimacy with the divine, are planted. Seeing dating in the context of this larger picture is helpful to understanding both the spiritual and Christian potential within these unique relationships.

Dating is, very simply and profoundly, a clue to life's mystery.

Dating Strengthens Our Spiritual Life

 I (Jason) used to live with two roommates, Jon and Tod. Through the course of living together for over two years, we came up with some rules about dating. Some were pretty basic: If a woman is engaged, you cannot try to go out with her. If a woman is living with her boyfriend, you cannot go out with her. If she is married, you cannot go out with her.

The rest were a little unique. Jon said that neither Tod nor I could date his significant other, Amy, even if he died. He threatened to haunt us if we did. Tod tried to insist that no first date should last more than six hours, but he was the only one who ever had problems with this issue. I insisted that any "making out" should be done in the person's own room. I kept shouting, "Get a room," but Jon undercut my rule by adding, "One with a window!" Louise, Tod's Danish girlfriend, tried to limit "snuggling" to only one hour a day.

We (both Jason and Donna) don't believe these rules by themselves are particularly helpful in understanding dating, though as silly as they sound, many of them were good rules. What do we mean by "good rules"? Good rules are usually dependent upon our understanding of what is good — for ourselves, for others, for our relationships, our communities. Even Jesus said that all the "rules" of the Old Testament pointed to something greater, namely love (Matthew 22:40). Thus, good rules, no matter how useful and structured they may be, point to something deeper and more mysterious. Even the roommate rules listed above have moral underpinnings.

For Christians, the something deeper involves living our lives in a way that fosters love. Thus, for those of us who date, we are called to date in such a way that it strengthens our spiritual life.

We claim that a good way to understand dating is as a clue to a mystery, an occasion for transformation, or part of our larger life journeys. What you should notice about these metaphors is that dating is not the whole picture. It is part of something greater. Often we think of dating as heading us toward marriage. For many of us, it is also a normal part of growing up — a place in life where we learn about and experience others and ourselves in a particularly focused and intimate way. We, however, believe that in addition to these elements, dating is also part of our spiritual lives.

What is a spiritual life? To put it as clearly as we can, a spiritual life is a person who lives life in such a way that God's love or the pursuit of ultimate meaning provides the foundation of her or his actions in the world. Examples of this are plentiful. You have the traditional figures of St. Peter and St. Paul. Peter's leadership in the early church was grounded in his love of God (Matthew 16:17–19). Paul's mission to the Gentiles was rooted in his zealousness to show himself worthy of God's love (Acts 9:15). Beyond these biblical figures, there is the brainy St. Thomas Aquinas whose massive philosophical outpourings were a consequence of his relationship with God. As a result of their love for the Creator, Martin Luther King Jr. was moved to address social injustices in the United States and Dorothy Day felt called to take care of the needy by establishing homes for people across the U.S.

On the contemporary and popular front, a friend of ours, Cara, suggested two musicians, Bono and Lauryn Hill, as good examples of spiritual lives. Of Bono, Cara commented, "Bono shatters the common conception of the flawless, 'cookie-cutter' Christian and has lived a life of purpose and intention according to his faith. He's been in a long, happy marriage and continues to use his gifts to benefit the world on many different levels." Of Lauryn Hill, Cara discussed the message in Hill's lyrics: "Listening to *The Miseducation of Lauryn Hill* is comparable to listening to any contemporary Christian album, yet it is something more than this, too. Like Bono, Hill uses music as a tool to explore her spirituality, as catharsis, and to testify to others. In her music, she openly admits to her mistakes, shortcomings, doubts, etc., but always incorporates her faith to show that everything can have a positive outcome." Our list of spiritual lives could go on and on. If it did it would be filled with martyrs, schoolteachers, married men and women, children, young people, as well as other rock stars.

The way we cultivate our relationship with God and our spiritual lives can take on many forms. Dating can be one of them. It is an expression of a particular type of love and an openness to communicating that love. Dating provides us one avenue for strengthening our spiritual lives.

Our contemporary understanding of dating is rather casual and involves an extensive freedom to date who we want, as much as we want (or at least as much as the other person wants), as long as we want to (as opposed to restricting our dating to *one* short period of courtship prior to marriage). Most of us today experience up to two decades or even more of "eligibility" to date. With regard to the way we date today, we do not exactly have many examples of dating saints or famous dating ministers to look up to. We do, however, have examples of saints whose actions can be used as analogies for dating and understanding how dating relates to the spiritual life and Christian faith — even with our contemporary approach to dating.

In the New Testament, we are introduced to the sisters Mary and Martha. Occasionally they disagree, as when Martha complains about Mary not helping out with the house (Luke 10:40), but both professed faith in Jesus: "Even now I know that whatever you ask of God, God will give you" (John 11:22). They were committed followers of Jesus, but they did not leave their daily activities behind. Instead, they made their home available to Jesus and his fellow travelers. They continued with their daily activities. Yet after meeting Jesus, they saw these same actions as graced by God. They started to see all that they did in this light and thereby cultivated their relationship with God. This is why Jesus loved Mary and Martha (John 11:5).

To take a more recent example, St. Elizabeth Ann Seton was born into a wealthy New York family. She married, had two sons and three daughters, was widowed, became poor, opened a school at the request of a bishop, started a society to care for widows and small children, set up a religious community, became its superior, and established several hospitals, orphanages, and schools. In her spare time, she wrote music and books. Not bad. What is most impressive about her is not that she had a strong spiritual life, but that her spiritual life led her into so many different activities. Elizabeth's spiritual life was grounded in, connected to, and inspired by her everyday experiences and encounters with others. Most of the other figures we mentioned had a single task set before them — church leader, activist, scholar — and accomplished their task with great enthusiasm. Elizabeth, on the other hand, did several different things. She did one task and when it was done, she moved on to the next. When it was done, she moved on again. No matter what she did, all her actions reflected her strong relationship with God, her spiritual life.

The examples of Mary, Martha, and Elizabeth give us two insights for understanding how dating strengthens our spiritual lives. First, Mary and Martha's show us that it is not necessarily what we do that strengthens our spiritual life but how we do it. The everyday lives of Mary and Martha were the same both before and after they met Jesus. However, after this encounter, their everyday activities were inspired by God's presence and became avenues of loving others and expressing their love of God. Likewise, dating for Christians must cultivate our relationship with and our love of God. On the surface, dating might look ordinary and common, but Christians are called to approach dating as an expression of love — love of God and love of neighbor — just as the everyday actions of Mary and Martha expressed their love of God.

Elizabeth's life gives us a second insight. She shows us that the life long commitment of a spiritual life is to God. Our activities, whatever diverse forms they take, are what build up this commitment and, ultimately, our capacity to express love of others. Thus, dating helps strengthen our life long commitment to and love of God, even though dating is neither a life long activity nor a life long commitment to the person we date. We should not confuse dating with the entirety of the spiritual life, but it can be an essential part. It is like one of the many activities that Elizabeth did, each potentially valuable and special in its own right. Just as setting up hospitals or schools or writing books and songs did for Elizabeth, dating can transform us and bring us closer to God.

Thus, if we are called to date, we are called to do so in a way that enables us to love God, our neighbors, and ourselves better. Dating is an activity that uniquely reveals how God's presence, love, and inspiration might be expressed in our everyday life. It provides us with a special opportunity to express our love of God in the company of another person.

Sometimes dinner, a movie, and a kiss good night can go further than we think.

A Brief Caveat about Spirituality and *Not* Dating

 After all our talk about spirituality *and* dating you might be thinking, "Well, what about spirituality and *not* dating?" What about spiritual development through other avenues? Or what if you don't date right now? What if you choose not to date? What if you just have not found anyone you are interested in? What if you happen to agree with the perspective that as a Christian you should wait to date until dating is really courtship?

What if? What if?!!! Good questions.

You may be getting the impression that we believe the only way you can experience the spiritual growth we describe here is through dating. That is not at all what we are trying to say. While we don't agree with the perspective that "the best preparation for marriage is to have no prior experience with relationships at all" or advocate this ideal as a rule for everyone, neither are we saying that you must date in order to adequately prepare yourself for marriage and to grow spiritually.

So what exactly are we saying then?

We are not saying that EVERYBODY needs to go out and date — that dating is a necessary part of a spiritual journey for everyone. We are saying that a rule that says every Christian must abstain from dating is unreasonable and underestimates the possibilities for spiritual, personal, and relational growth in dating.

We're offering an alternative perspective for people about dating. We hope to convey that, as a rule, the prescription for total abstention from dating does not work for all young people. Just because you go out with someone does not mean that you are going against God or that you have to separate your dating relationship from your spiritual life. We also believe that if you choose *not* to go out with anyone, this does not mean that you are going against God or stunting your spiritual growth.

When it comes down to it, there are many right paths, not just one acceptable road for all. We want to open up the options. We're offering an alternative perspective to the one offered by so many Christian authors. We believe that if you do meet someone you would like to go out with, and she or he does not turn out to be the person that you marry, or if you date someone and you are not even thinking about marriage at that point in life, then you are not straying down the wrong path or going against "what God wants."

We want to open up the conversation on Christianity, spirituality, and dating. We believe that going out on dates is a viable choice for a Christian, one that does not require you to distance your relationships from your spiritual life. In fact, dating can enhance your spiritual life and growth. Up till now, for young Christians the only option seemed to be waiting for courtship and staying away from dating; that was promoted as the right path for every unmarried person. We just don't think that it is the right path for everybody. But we do think that it may be the right path for some.

Several New York University students questioned us on this very issue.

"So you guys are totally against Joshua Harris, huh?" one of them asked over dinner one night.

Wait a minute. Yes and no. No and yes.

OK, we are not "against" Joshua Harris. Yes, we offer a critique of his book, but we are not trying to get you to throw his perspective out the window. We realize that his perspective makes sense and gives guidance to a lot of people who read his books. What we disagree with is the way that he presents his opinion, as if it is the only right way: kissing dating good-bye is what God wants for all unmarried people.

Our answer to this, as you already know, is *no*. Kissing dating good-bye is not the only "right way." After all, "there are different kinds of spiritual gifts but the same spirit; there are different forms of service but the same Lord; there are different workings but the same God who produces all of them in everyone" (1 Corinthians 12:4–6).

While a lot of people we talked to challenged us on this issue, Kristen is the person who really pushed us to answer the challenge more fully. We really don't want you to walk away from this book thinking that we are against not-dating.

We are not *anti-not-dating*. So, there you go.

Glad that we got that cleared up.

Spiritualizing Sex

This section is key to all of what we are saying about dating. We know this because every time we bring up the topic of dating and spirituality in conversation, everyone automatically wants to know what we think of sex. Jumping immediately to the topic of sexuality is not a surprise, given both everyone's immersion in pop culture today and popular religion's very public preoccupation with sex outside of marriage. As we said before, everybody wants to reduce dating to sex.

The zillion-dollar question, of course, becomes this: if dating is different than friendship because of eros, does eros limit or even eliminate the potential compatibility of dating and our spiritual lives?

As you will see in the section that follows, our answer is "no." Kissing can be valuable because it expresses our love for another in a concrete way. Sex can be good if it builds up the couple's love for each other, strengthens their resolve to love their neighbor, and solidifies their commitment to God. Chastity can be understood as the level of sexual expression that corresponds with the level of commitment in a relationship. Even one's prayer life can lead to a greater understanding of physical intimacy just as one's physical intimacy can lead to a greater understanding of one's relationship with God.

Notice that we are not concerned with spelling out the "law" or the dos and don'ts of sexuality. Instead, we are concerned with the *attitude* by which we approach the sexual dimension of dating relationships. We're articulating a spirituality of sexuality in dating as opposed to a morality.

Again, here's something you should know about our perspectives before moving on. We both agree that kissing and sex and all things in between can lead a person to greater love of self, neighbor, and God and that sexual activity needs to be measured against the commitment of the relationship. We also believe that the act of sexual intercourse requires a loving, committed relationship: casual sex is far from what we advocate. Although we agree that with intercourse love and commitment are necessary, we differ a bit regarding the type of commitment. On the one hand, I (Jason) believe intercourse is intimately connected to procreation and thus the commitment necessary is marriage. I (Donna), on the other hand, do not agree that the only place for sexual intercourse is a marital relationship. I believe the love and commitment necessary for sex is possible in circumstances other than marriage, especially since both our society and religion restricts many couples from marriage altogether.

You will see both of these views expressed in the following pages.

The Value of Kissing

Why do human beings kiss? It is not necessary for our survival. It does not meet any biological need or help us find shelter, food, or water. We do not even need it to reproduce. Yet kissing is wonderful. It feels valuable to us. Married couples kiss almost absentmindedly to express their love. When we are sad, our friends and family will often comfort us with a kiss. We greet friends that we have not seen for a while with a kiss. We go to reunions where we have to kiss any number of relatives. In dating, kissing usually implies that there is at least some spark or attraction between the two people.

Almost all of us remember our first romantic kiss and the euphoria that followed it.

At first glance, it may seem that we kiss for a number of different reasons. Just from the examples above, friends kiss to console and to celebrate, family to affirm their bonds, and couples to express feelings of romance or falling in love. Underneath this diversity, however, is a unity: kissing expresses love and affection. We are fond of and love not only our romantic interests but also our friends and family. For sure, we kiss our friends and family differently than our lovers, since when kissing a romantic interest, a kiss usually also expresses attraction. Even though the way we kiss can carry additional meanings, at the least, each act communicates an affirmation of and a hope for another's good, what we call love.

Kissing is, thus, a wonderful expression of love and affection because, at its best, it affirms a love for the whole person. It encompasses two fundamental aspects of human existence: the physical and the spiritual.

On a spiritual level, human beings all desire love, friendship, and companionship. We may need to be by ourselves at times, we may (rightly) choose being alone as opposed to being in a bad relationship, but we almost always enjoy being in a good relationship, hanging out with our friends, and even at times talking to our parents.

Yet this spiritual connection, as spirituality is often understood, is not sufficient by itself. As physical creatures, our expressions of love need to have a physical dimension. Our spirituality needs to have a physical dimension.

In the way spirituality is typically understood, spirituality is separated from the physical. We do not often see the spiritual as grounded in an embrace, a cry, or the taste of good food. We tend to view the spiritual as almost an "out-of-body" realm. Instead, we must learn that the spiritual and physical are intertwined. It is through our bodily experiences — that which connects us to the world and to others — that we develop a sense of spirituality in our lives and a connection to the divine.

By the "physical" dimension of love, we are not yet talking about something as profound as sex either. We are talking about something more basic and fundamental to relationships.

We need physical interactions with those we love. E-mailing our friends is great, but it is not the same as hanging out with them. Talking to our family helps to keep in contact, but it does not replace the joys (and irritations) of actually being with them. Scientific research suggests that babies need coddling and physical affection for proper development. Touching, hugging, holding hands, standing close together — humans need this type of contact to help themselves and their relationships flourish.

Christianity affirms the importance of both the physical and spiritual elements in our relations with others. It calls people not only to pray for but also to feed, clothe, and shelter our neighbors. It claims that we cannot genuinely love our neighbors if we do not attend to their physical needs. On a deeper level, the fact that God took on physical existence (i.e., became human) implies that our connection to God and the spiritual world is precisely through our corporeal natures. To reject bodily existence is to reject a fundamental belief in Christianity. The Dorothy Days and Mother Teresas of the world are affirmations of the unity of the physical and the spiritual, living out this connection in their lifelong work helping and loving others or attending compassionately to their physical needs.

If the physical and spiritual dimensions within all our relationships are inherently intertwined, then this also must be true of our romantic relationships in particular. We definitely need people who genuinely care about us, respect us, and are concerned about our good. But we also need concrete expressions of these sentiments. We are bodily creatures and come to know the world and others through our bodily senses. Genuine love takes both the physical and spiritual into account.

Love and spirituality are connected. The body and spirituality are connected. Kissing mediates the spiritual through the physical. So it naturally follows that expressions of bodily love are also expressions of spirituality, and kissing is valuable because it binds these two elements together. Through physical touching, kissing affirms that one's attractions, sentiments, or love is real. It mingles joy, love, and pleasure together. It is a gift.

Still, we do not want to claim too much for kissing. Although it does mean something, it does not mean *everything*. A kiss is not the be all and end all of love. It often just signifies the beginnings of love or attraction. To a certain degree, Frank Sinatra was right when he crooned, "Sometimes a kiss is just a kiss." Kissing obviously does not imply that two people are hopelessly and forever in love. All we are claiming is that kissing must, at the least, stem from mutual and genuine affection.

Sadly most of us know of instances where a kiss has not been intended as good or has not been an experience intertwining the physical and the spiritual. We may have kissed or been kissed by someone where the only desire was for the pleasure that comes from kissing. The kiss only affirmed the physical aspect of love. Not that physical pleasure is bad, but taken by itself it decouples our physical existence from our spiritual one. We become only half human instead of being a complete "physically spiritual" being.

We may have also kissed or been kissed by someone where the act was not a true expression of our or the other's feelings. The kiss was intended for something other than an affirmation of love or affection. People have tried to use kissing to get others to do what they want or move others to accept them. The former is a type of manipulation. The latter often results from our need to conform to another's desire so they will like us, accept us, or stay with us.

Christians know at least one example where kissing has been used wrongly: "Jesus said to him, 'Judas, are you betraying the Son of Man with a kiss?'" (Luke 22:48). Judas took an action that is supposed to reflect our love and respect of another and used it to bring about the destruction of this person. Judas's act adds wrong to wrong by betraying Jesus through the betrayal of the meaning of kissing. In such cases, kissing is devalued. It is turned from a spiritual, physical expression of love and affection into a means to some other end, like control or profit. The truly dangerous consequence of devaluing kissing is that it devalues the human person. Kissing becomes the tool to manipulate people for some other end. Instead of the person being the highest good and kissing affirming this good, the human and the kiss become utensils for manipulation or the exertion of power.

Still, all of these possible dangers are trumped by the more fundamental and frequent reality of the value of kissing. Kissing is good. It expresses a love that encompasses the whole person, body and spirit. And these sentiments are no small matter.

The moral of the story is that just because you are a Christian person or a spiritual person, does not mean that you cannot kiss someone you like. In fact, in kissing we find elements of the spiritual and the Christian. Kissing expresses love, and this expression is the value of kissing.

A Different View of Chastity

 "There's a sexual revolution going on in America, and believe it or not, it has nothing to do with Christina Aguilera's bare-it-all video *Dirrty*. The uprising is taking place in the real world, not on *The Real World*. Visit any American high school and you'll likely find a growing number of students who watch scabrous TV shows like *Shipmates,* listen to Eminem — and have decided to remain chaste until marriage."[6]

What does "chaste until marriage" mean today? At one of our talks on dating, Robert Barry, a professor from Providence College, asked a similar question, but asked it in the context of its relevance to dating.[7] He wondered whether we could define chastity in the context of a dating relationship.

We started asking ourselves: What would be the physical and emotional boundaries for "chaste dating?" Is "chaste dating" a realistic possibility? How would we know the limits of chastity to set in a relationship that is not friendship yet not marriage either?

These questions are tough to answer but important to ask in exploring the relationship between spirituality and dating, particularly if you are a Christian trying to negotiate the sexual dimension of a romantic relationship.

The *Newsweek* article quoted above did not help us to answer these questions. The article shared a range of opinions about "chaste until marriage." It included interviews with a young woman who has never been kissed and has no interest in being kissed, a guy and girl who are dating but are not having sex, and another guy who already has had sex, yet is currently abstaining. The parents of the guy and girl who are dating even tried to quantify some rules for the couple, advising that there is "no touching anywhere a soccer uniform covers." The author of the article also talks to a "ring-bearer," a young Christian who participates in a ceremony at church where she receives a ring to be worn on the ring finger of the left hand (like a wedding ring), signifying a commitment to remain a virgin until marriage.

This ambiguity in the use of the term *chastity* — from not kissing to no sex to *no more* sex — made us realize that to understand chastity in dating, we needed to understand chastity itself.

Historically the word *chaste* has been associated with Catholic priests, monks, and nuns, since they all take a vow of chastity when ordained. This particular vow of chastity signifies a commitment to abstain from sex for the rest of one's life. Another common association with the word *chastity*, which has taken on a humorous tone for most of us today, is the ever-famous chastity belt. Historically the chastity belt was a locked contraption designed to preserve the virginity of the unfortunate women who were forced to wear them, either forever or at least until they were married.

The above perspectives tend to define chastity as connected primarily with virginity: chastity equals not engaging in sexual activity. Yet this view of chastity is not the only one.

In his book *The Good News about Sex and Marriage*, Christopher West bemoans the often negative connotations people have with regard to sexuality and chastity. He describes the virtue of chastity as "essential if we are to discover and fulfill the very meaning of our being and existence," including sexual expression in appropriate circumstances, i.e., marital relationships.

Looking back to the early centuries of the Christian church, even St. Augustine proffered an interpretation of chastity that included sexual expression. For Augustine, the gift of marriage was God's way of giving humanity an avenue to deal with the human sex drive and to procreate without sinning. Thus, a chaste marriage is not one where sex does not occur but is one where sex is done for the right reason, which for Augustine was having children. (Though even in marriage, Augustine believed that sex was sinful to a degree.)

Most Christian denominations proclaim the value of chaste sex within marriage. Catholicism, for example, argues that marriage can be chaste if it is done for the mutual benefit of the partners, just as long as it is still open to procreation. Other denominations recognize that sex in marriage can enhance, support, and develop the love between the couple even if every single act is not open to children. Thus, loving sex is chaste sex, and chastity means something more than "not having sex."

What then is chastity? We understand it in terms of faithfulness to a commitment.

This faithfulness is precisely what links the chastity of the ordained and the chastity of the marriage. Through ordination, a priest vows fidelity to and love of God, and this commitment is at least partially expressed in the commitment to abstain from all sexual activity. Likewise, in a marriage a couple takes a vow of chastity. The vow of chastity in Christian marriage involves a commitment that within the relationship, each person pledges their fidelity to the other on many different levels, including physically and emotionally. At least within the Catholic tradition, a "chaste" marriage permits sexual activity as long as it occurs within the context of a loving and lifelong commitment that at some point includes the possibility of having and raising children.

It is with regard to the concept of chastity *outside* of marriage with which many Christian theologians and popular writers alike, as well as some parents, pastors, and fellow religious teachers, struggle. The Christian teaching about chastity outside of marriage is generally abstention from *all* sexual activity. There is either marriage *or* platonic friendship.

Though Christopher West works to offer a positive interpretation of the relationship between sexuality and chastity in his book, he permits this positive relationship only within the context of marriage. Like many other Christian authors, he defines sex only in terms of intercourse, and proclaims that any sexual activity outside of marriage is also outside of love. Loving sexual expression is impossible unless one is married. Engaging in sexual expression in dating turns out to be going against Christ and the Christian faith altogether.

We believe that "chaste" dating for Christians is possible, if we explore further the understanding of chastity in terms of faithfulness to a commitment. We regard chastity in dating, at a foundational level, as doing what is appropriate given the level of commitment in a relationship — physically, morally, spiritually, as well as sexually.

Determining the level of commitment, though, can be very difficult. This is the challenge we face in trying to determine what chastity means in the context of a relationship that is most likely finite. In commitments that are meant to be lifelong, such as in marriage or becoming a priest, it is much easier to determine how to appropriately express our level of commitment to the relationship. Deciding to engage in sexual intercourse with someone you intend to spend the rest of your life with is obviously different than doing so with someone with whom you may only spend one month.

Yet we can at least begin to understand chastity in dating relationships by saying that the level of sexual interaction between two people will vary as the level of commitment in dating varies. After all, there are people you go out with only once. There are people you go out with a few times but do not consider the relationship serious. There are people you date exclusively for only a few months. There are even people that you date exclusively for several years. What is appropriate in a relationship that has gone on for six years, been accepted by both families is very different than a relationship that is one month old. There are probably an uncountable number of permutations of these different levels as well, almost all of which, in dating, do not turn out to be lifelong in nature.

With regard to how we go about determining the role of sexual activity in dating relationships, the *Newsweek* article claims that the question of whether or not to have sex, the degree to which one engages in sexual activity, or the choice to remain "chaste" is "an extraordinarily private decision." Yet, from what we are saying above, chastity within a dating relationship is not solely a private decision for many reasons. The first reason is obvious, and relates to what we said in "Making Dating Meaningful" about the reciprocal relationship of experience and reflection, communication and the spiritual dimensions of dating. Dating relationships require communication between the two people involved. Determining the level of commitment in dating — and thus determining the level of acceptable sexual activity — is something that must occur between those two people. It is a topic that must become a "public" discussion within the context of the relationship. One member of the couple cannot "privately" determine that he or she will be having sex. While each member of the couple certainly may feel differently about the role of sex in the relationship, ultimately, he or she must be willing to communicate about this issue with the other, coming to a joint decision about how the sexual dimension of the relationship will be expressed between them. It is a *communal* decision in this way.

It is also a communal decision because sexual activity affects the couple's relationships with their parents, peers, friends, and siblings. How the couple communicates their activities to these other people raises issues of honesty, trust, and dependability. Thus, any decision the couple makes about sexuality must take into account the fact that it will affect not just the two making the decision but also the many people who care about them.

In addition, determining appropriate sexual activity in dating relationships is communal due to the potential consequences of sexual activity that we must all consider. These consequences have physical, spiritual, and ethical implications. Engaging in sexual activity, to any degree, can put us at risk to sexually transmitted disease. Engaging in sexual intercourse can result in pregnancy — an intense reality that a couple cannot afford to ignore and, in dating relationships, are normally not equipped to deal with. Engaging in sexual activity has religious and spiritual implications. Our religious communities, our families, and as a result, many of us, have particular expectations for ourselves that are important to consider in determining the appropriate level of sexual activity in a dating relationship.

Chastity in dating is far from an extraordinarily private decision — determining what chastity means in dating is communal in nature. "Chaste" dating depends upon how committed two people are to each other. The level of commitment is discerned by the type of dating relationship we decide it to be, the way the relationship impacts us and the person we date, as well as the implications the relationship has for us in terms of health, ethics, religion, as well as our other relationships.

The view of chastity we are proposing, a view that is compatible with dating, is not a set of rules about what to do and what not to do. Instead it involves a faithfulness to the kind of relationship you have. Determining the level of commitment is not easy. It involves the consideration of many different issues. It involves asking yourself in company with your partner: What kind of relationship do we wish to have? How is it appropriate to express our relationship in its sexual dimension? What about the consequences of sexual activity in our relationship physically? Ethically? Religiously?

It takes all of these questions and many more to understand chastity in dating. Chastity in dating is not easy to determine, but we believe it is possible to do so, and worthwhile to try. Addressing the question of chastity in dating will at least give us a place from which we can struggle with the issue of sexuality within our dating relationships.

When Sex Is Good

When I (Jason) was in graduate school, I had a rough time. I was struggling to write my dissertation. I was working full-time. Most of my friends that I had been in school with had left town. I was feeling lonely and doubting my ability to finish the degree. This was when I started going out with Kelly.

I remember the first time we kissed. I suddenly felt loved. Not that I was *not* loved at the time. My friends and family all cared about me. I knew in my mind that God loved me. But through the kiss I "felt" love, and not just Kelly's affection but the love of God working through her. This experience, as small as it may seem, gave me more confidence in myself and strengthened my resolve to finish school. Kelly obviously was not intending these consequences nor was I really looking for them. They resulted unexpectedly from the kiss.

Is this a story about sex? True, it does not involve the act of sexual intercourse, but it does involve an attitude toward sexuality that extends beyond what we often understand as "sex." As we noted in earlier essays, a typical attitude about sex we encounter in both culture and institutional religion often reduces sex to the act of intercourse. Yet our attitude about sexuality views the one-on-one physical interaction in a relationship as not just any act of love but an act of love that builds up people and their faith. We are talking about a love emerging from one's attraction and bodily expression that is open and leads to something greater. It is an attitude that gives us the ability to see when the act of sex is good. So, yes, it is a story about sex, a good story.

Our culture also has an attitude toward sex. Occasionally, but not often, we see sexuality portrayed with just a kiss, most notably in Meg Ryan and Tom Hanks movies. More frequently we encounter the alluring look of oversexed models on the covers of

Vogue and *Cosmo*. We see commercials that associate sexy, beautiful women and men with everything from soap to cars to beer (of course). We watch movies that have sexy people flirting with each other. (They usually end up sleeping together, of course, but we usually do not see *it*, the act of sex. We mostly see the kissing, the etc., etc., that leads to the act that follows it.)

The most explicit portrayals of sex might be found in the junk e-mails we get in our Hotmail or AOL accounts. They range from offering pornographic pictures to sex techniques to medical treatments that will improve one's sex appeal. (For me [Jason], the number of e-mails I receive offering to improve my sexual performance is only rivaled by the ones promising financial security. I wonder sometimes if both of these are targeted to me because I am a theology professor?)

The message seems to be: free love for everybody.

As we discussed in previous essays, our culture views sex primarily in terms of pleasure and hence something one should "do." This principle is not explicitly taught in our culture; rather, it is presumed. Our culture assumes the belief "sex feels good, so do it" is the way that everyone does (or should) view sex and everything related to sex. The only stipulation is that all the parties involved must freely consent to what is going on.

We are uncomfortable with this perspective. The problem with "all sex is good so do it" lies in how the concept of "good" is defined: as pleasure in its most superficial sense. It does not take much reflection to see problems with this position. It might feel good to get the four-dollar caramel macchiato with extra whipped cream every day, but it is probably not good for our health, weight, or even finances. We may feel good in the trendy $2,000 outfit, but trendy might not be so practical with our bank accounts and the outfit may be "not-so-trendy" sooner rather than later anyway. Pleasure is not always the best measure of goodness.

In addition, when pleasure is the highest or only good it limits our ability to pursue any good that is not immediately satisfying. Thus, "sex feels good, so do it" can divorce our physical actions from their higher purposes in life, our spiritual life. And, as we have said time and time again in this book, the physical and the spiritual are inextricably intertwined.

Some Christians, of course, also have this attitude toward sex: "sex feels good, so *don't* do it." They view self-deprivation as virtuous and more significant than engaging in activity that brings us physical and, usually, sinful pleasure. People are not supposed to enjoy their sexuality — we are supposed to view it as appropriate mainly for the purpose of procreation. We end up with the impression that outside of marriage almost anything more than a quick peck on the lips is questionable. It might indeed be pleasurable now, but it only leads to the fires of hell later.

Of course, as we discussed in "A Different View of Chastity," there are legitimate reasons to have concerns about sexual activity occurring casually and/or outside of a long-term commitment — the consequences of sexual activity can have a serious impact on our health, our futures, the future of any children produced, and our sense of connection and faithfulness to our religious tradition. Yet we believe that the discomfort of some Christians with regard to sex extends beyond concerns for the consequences of sexual activity. It points to an overall discomfort with sexuality in general (even within marriage) and leads to a rejection of all sexual expression outside of a lifelong commitment.

Like the cultural perspective, we are uncomfortable with this Christian one. Its understanding of "sexuality" is problematic because its frequent rejection of all sexuality often leads us to view others as suspicious or dangerous, and pleasure and our bodies as sinful. Since many of us are waiting well into our thirties to get married, this initial suspicion of others can easily develop into a permanent way of viewing the world, and potentially a deep embarrassment and discomfort among young women and men with their bodies and sexual expression.

In addition, this type of Christian "sexuality" disconnects love from the body. Sexual expression is either banned or hindered. People can fall in love, true, but should not act on it. The body becomes an unacceptable, sinful means of expressing love. The only true expression must stand outside of the physical realm.

A Christian should find these conclusions troubling. Viewing other people as dangerous or as temptations goes expressly against Jesus' vision: "Lord, when did we see our hungry and feed you, or thirsty and give you drink? When did we see you a stranger and welcome you, or naked and clothe you? When did we see you ill or in prison, and visit you? . . . 'Amen, I say to you, whatever you did for one of these least brothers of mine, you did for me' " (Matthew 25:37–40). Others should be viewed not as dangerous but as God in disguise.

Similarly Christians should not accept that bodily expression is sinful. As we have said, a love disconnected from the body is not a fully spiritual love. Jesus not only prayed for people but also cured their physical ailments like sickness, lameness, blindness, and deafness (Luke 7:21–23). Moreover, God did not express love for humanity through a disembodied love, but instead through a human being who lived and died as a human being, uniting divinity to humanity. Even today, we would think someone pretty strange who believed that loving your neighbor had nothing to do with feeding the hungry, giving drink to the thirsty, getting help for the sick, or visiting the lonely. While sexual expression is not feeding the hungry, it is a form of bodily expression designed to communicate the love of another. Humans are capable of expressing love in many ways, including sexually.

Young Christians today often feel faced with the choice of being a Christian and totally rejecting popular culture's embrace of sexuality or accepting the popular view and totally rejecting

Christianity. We believe that this is a false choice. We think there is another option.

Our perspective on sex — that it is a physical, romantic interaction that builds up people and their faith, that emerges from one's attraction and bodily expression, and is open and leads to something greater — is not foreign to the Christian faith. Our view is echoed by a number of theologians today, including Dorothee Soelle and Elisabeth Moltmann-Wendel in particular.

In *To Work and to Love,* Dorothee Soelle envisions sex as "a sacrament, a sign of grace in bodily element. . . . Human sexuality may be understood as a sacramental reality in which the word of love comes to the element of the flesh and interprets its meaning. The sexual act, then, becomes a sign of God's grace."[8] She also contends that sexual expression is central to our "lifelong challenge to become fully human."

Elisabeth Moltmann-Wendel offers a similar perspective in *I Am My Body: A Theology of Embodiment.* For her, sexual expression through the body is nothing to be ashamed or afraid of. It should instead be encountered as a *gift* (much like the love of another person). Humans have been given the gift of touch from God — a very special language of love.[9]

The above perspective on sex contends that our relationship to our sexuality should be integrated into our relationship with God and, when this integration occurs, sex is good. Bodily expressions of love are signs of God's grace. Our relationship to our sexuality should be lifelong in nature. It is part of what it means to be human and Christian. We learn about it when we are young and begin to ask questions about how we all got here, and become healthily curious about it when we start to feel attraction for others in junior high and high school. Sexual expression is not something that we need to place in a deep dark corner of who we are. If we combine these conclusions with everything else in this essay, we arrive at a fuller perspective of the limited situations where sex can be good.

First, of course, sexual expression must stem from mutual, free consent. Our cultural emphasis on freedom and choice do tell us something valuable. Unfortunately, it often stops with this point. Christians, however, need more. Thus, sexual expression is also good when it strengthens one's view of other people as good. Jesus called us to see others as God in disguise. So if sexuality is part of dating and dating part of the life of a Christian, then sexuality should foster a view of the world where others are seen as gift. To put it negatively, sex is not good when it stems from manipulation or causes sorrow, pain, and suffering in another, when it hurts rather than helps another, when it is meaningless (casual) rather than meaningful.

Sexual expression is good when it connects the pleasure of physical intimacy with love and honest commitment to the nature of the relationship. Sex is good when it nourishes the spiritual life of the people involved. Sexuality that disturbs one's relationship with God, that inclines one to go against what is right and wrong, that overpowers all other dimensions of a romantic relationship, is not good.

Perhaps most importantly, sex is good when all of these components are combined. For a fully Christian sexuality, you need all of the above elements. A couple needs to consent to sexual expression, consider the consequences of sexual expression on many levels, and should intend to do what is good for the other person. With these issues taken into account, physical intimacy can turn out to not only to enrich our lives, relationships, and experiences of our bodies, but also lead us to become better Christians.

Sexual expression is a *good* part of dating.

Spiritual Intimacy

Julian is someone we admire. She is extremely intelligent, an excellent and engaging writer, a leader in her community, and a deeply committed Christian. She is one of those people whose spiritual commitment is inspiring and often life-changing to those who come into contact with her; she challenges where we stand in our faith and spiritual development. Even if you only interact with her once or twice, she leaves a lasting impression. You walk away thinking, "Wow, what an amazing woman!"

One of the most impressive things about Julian is her sense of spiritual intimacy with others and with God. For Julian, the experience of being an embodied person is central to her spirituality. She is sophisticated in her sense of the body as central to her capacity for relationship with God. For Julian, spirituality is a "sensual" thing. Her spirituality exemplifies the role that the body can play in our spiritual growth toward God. This, of course, is what many Christian scholars write about today in an attempt to overcome our tendency to divorce spirituality from everything bodily, especially our sexuality.

Go Julian — modern woman in our midst. Sort of.

The Julian we are talking about is better known as Julian of Norwich, a fourteenth-century Christian mystic from England. That's right. *Fourteenth century. Mystic.*

It might be difficult to imagine that a medieval woman mystic would have something to teach us in the twenty-first century about our bodies and spirituality. Many Christians and non-Christians alike understand spirituality as an "outside of the body" experience, especially when the case is mystical union with God. This union is often described as the ultimate out of body spiritual experience — an experience of union with God that is world rejecting and body rejecting.

So what are we doing then, using a *mystic* to talk about intimacy?

Feminist philosopher Grace Jantzen describes Julian's perspective on spirituality in relation to the body in the following way: "Spirituality [for Julian] does not mean leaving part of the self behind, but bringing the whole of the self, sensuality included, into the unity of the love of God in which she believes we are enfolded."[10] Loving God, for Julian, requires the whole body, sensuality and all. Many feminist writers on women mystics contend that an understanding of mysticism as a non-bodily experience is based on mistaken interpretations of mystical experience.

It is true, though, that Julian's perspective on the body in her spiritual experiences and relationship with God is unusual for the fourteenth century, but it is becoming less and less unusual in discussions on spirituality today. There is a powerful movement occurring within Christianity today that is directed toward "recovering" the body in our spiritual lives with feminist theologians and philosophers like Jantzen, Soelle, and Moltmann-Wendel (mentioned in the previous essay) who write on this topic.

In addition, the other reason we bring up mysticism is because at its foundation mysticism is all about intimacy. It is about the ultimate intimacy of all — total union, total intimacy — between a person and God.

Scholars of mystical theology tend to describe mysticism as a journey or path consisting of several stages. At each stage, a person gets closer and closer to union of the self with God. Along the way, a person experiences sacrifice, at times darkness, and at other moments, joy and reassurance. The mystical journey is not a perfect journey — it is a journey with bumps along the road. But ultimately it is a journey toward the total opening up of the self. The mystical path is about what it means to become vulnerable toward an *other*, and in the case of mysticism, one becomes totally vulnerable, completely open, to God and God's presence.

Due to the total openness and vulnerability of a person to God that is usually associated with mysticism, mystical experience has deep associations to ecstasy — spiritual ecstasy, that is. Spiritual or mystical ecstasy occurs when one experiences union of the self with God. For example, Hadewijch of Antwerp, another medieval woman mystic, vividly and sensually describes her encounter with God: "He came himself to me, took me entirely in his arms, and pressed me to him; and all my members felt his full felicity, in accordance with the desire of my heart and my humanity. So I was outwardly satisfied and fully transported."[11]

Very racy.

Sixteenth-century mystic St. Teresa of Avila's experience of mystical union is depicted in a famous sculpture by the artist Giovanni Bernini entitled *Ecstasy of St. Teresa*. Bernini depicts Teresa in what looks like sexual ecstasy. Mystical union and sexual intimacy, at least analogously, are often not that far apart for many mystics.

If we stop and think about it, this association makes sense. Where else in human experience do we so often talk about total vulnerability, total openness, total giving of one self to another but in sex? Probably one of the best examples of the total human giving of body and soul in a relationship is in the act of sex.

Metaphorically speaking, sexual union is a powerful and perhaps accurate metaphor for describing the experience of spiritual ecstasy.

What does all this talk of mystical ecstasy have to do with intimacy in dating? Are we promoting that you all go out and have sex because sexual union is something like union with God?

No.

We are noting the important role of the body and bodily expression to both spirituality and intimacy in our relationships. In opening ourselves up in relationships and becoming vulnerable to another person, we open ourselves to the experience of intimacy on many levels. In the case of mysticism, the "other" we become vulnerable to and intimate with is God. In a dating relationship, that "other" we open ourselves to in both body and soul is the person that we date. Experiences of intimacy with God can teach us about intimacy in our relationships with others, and what we learn from our intimate experiences with others can teach us to deepen our relationship to the divine.

We kiss, we hold, and we touch. That is part of how, as humans, we express like and love. In Bernini's statue of Teresa, we see Teresa physically reaching out with her body to God, expressing her total love and desire for God, loving God with body and soul intertwined. It is a powerful depiction of the way humans reach out to those we love and in turn how we may also reach out to the divine.

What does this mean for sexual intimacy in a dating relationship? Since sex is such a wonderful metaphor for spiritual intimacy and is an important way in which humans connect, shouldn't we have sex when we are dating? No.

So are we not to engage in sexual activity at all in dating? Again, no.

We aren't setting up rules here. Instead, we are inviting you to look at yourselves, especially your dating selves, in a new way. In a sense, we are inviting you to see yourselves and your relationships through a new pair of glasses. The glasses are not X-ray glasses that see through the body to the soul. Instead, they enable us to see the body itself as spiritual. Human beings are bodies, communication between people only happens through bodies, and, for Christians, it is the body of Christ that saves the whole person, the body-soul creatures that we are.

If we turn these glasses upon ourselves, we will see that we should respect our whole person. We must value our bodies because they are crucial to our human and spiritual flourishing, and since they are valuable, we should avoid anything that degrades the body-soul creatures that we are. We should *neither* jump into bed with every person we meet *nor* exclude bodily love from every relationship we have. Bodily expressions of love are one avenue through which we learn about intimacy on many levels. Here there is a need for couples to be honest and responsible — physically, emotionally, and spiritually — in choosing the level of intimacy appropriate in their respective relationship.

Spiritual intimacy brings together both our relationship to God and our relationship to the others. Spiritual intimacy involves our experience of the bodily and sexual intimacy that opens us to God, and an intimacy with God that leads to a better understanding of a couple's bodily and sexual expressions.

Dating in the Twenty-First Century

Dating emerged as a twentieth century phenomenon. It continues now in the twenty-first century where it evolves at a breakneck pace. It is hard to keep up. What with reality TV and all kinds of experimental Internet dating going on, the dating style of our parents seems as if it is from the Dark Ages. Whereas my (Donna's) Catholic mother might have cried bitter tears twenty-five years ago for my bringing home a Jewish boy, today she instead asks for a good book to learn about Judaism. Most of us do not even bat an eye when a Baptist dates a Methodist, and watching two men walk down the street hand in hand can be an everyday occurrence if you live in a big city like New York, San Francisco, or Washington, D.C.

In the section that follows we broaden our perspective by exploring the joys and challenges of interreligious dating and interdenominational dating, as well as the struggles that same-sex couples face today in seeking to understand their relationships in light of religion and spirituality.

Due to the fact that I (Donna) am dating a Jew, we decided to start with the issue of interreligious dating and explore the value of diversity in a relationship. For the other two essays, we turned to others for conversation, reflection, and advice. We asked a Catholic friend and an evangelical Protestant friend to talk about the ecumenical value, mutual enrichment, and difficulties of interdenominational dating. We talked with some gay and lesbian friends about the issues same-sex couples face with regard to religion and relationships. We also reflected on the importance of religious groups, Christianity in particular, facing and openly discussing same-sex relationships.

For me (Jason), some of the issues addressed in this section are in tension with my religious background. I am a Catholic and this tradition has nurtured me throughout my entire intellectual, spiritual, and social life. It would be much easier for me to ignore the above issues and exclude them from the book, yet I believe I must let these voices speak, think about what they have to say, and see where these challenges lead me in my understanding of relationships and faith.

For me (Donna), what we discuss in this section is particularly close to my heart, and not only because I am in an interreligious relationship. I firmly believe we can never predict with whom we are going to fall in love, and if we are so lucky to find love in this life, how in the world can someone or some group proclaim we are not allowed to express that love? I am well aware of the tensions that arise between Christianity and the type of relationships discussed in this section and do not mean to minimize them. Yet I also believe that none of us are so close to God that we can pretend to legislate love as if we were divine ourselves.

For some of our readers, this section will be cause for great resistance and struggle. For others the discussion will seem obvious.

We invite you to consider these issues where you are, remaining open to how they arise within the dating life today.

So You Celebrate Easter and He Celebrates Passover

As the seeds for this book were beginning to grow, we talked to many different groups, heard just about a million stories from people about their dating experiences, and fielded a ton of questions. One question, however, startled us. We were giving a talk on dating and spirituality at a conference. After the talk, we took questions from the audience.

One of the first questions was from a man, probably somewhere in his late twenties, sitting toward the front of the room.

"What do you think of 'dating outside the tribe'?" he asked both of us.

Dating outside the tribe? What did he mean by this exactly? What tribe was he talking about?

We asked him to explain his question a bit further. It turns out he was referring to Christians engaging in interfaith relationships. Did we think it was OK or should Christians not go out with someone of a different religious faith?

Little did the man know the irony of his asking this particular question given our audience that day.

We (Jason and Donna) eventually turned to each other and laughed.

Sitting at the back of the audience was our good friend and Donna's significant other, Josh. Josh is Jewish.

Well, there you go.

After explaining who was at the back of the room and Josh giving the audience a little wave and everyone having a nice chuckle, the man's question was easily and succinctly answered.

Sort of.

We realized after our talk that day that we needed to reflect further on this issue. How *do* we approach this relevant topic in talking about the relationship between spirituality and dating? What do we need to think about and say to our audience to offer some guidance on the question? Can dating someone of a different faith enhance our spiritual growth and journeys? Or, for some, is dating someone of a different faith simply not a viable option?

We live in a world filled with diversity, even if it doesn't always seem that way on the surface. Diversity comes in so many forms — it is part of what makes humanity and creation, so utterly incredible. There are all kinds of diversity in our lives: racial, economic, educational, ethnic, moral, political, geographical, and linguistic. We are all of different ages and have different levels, preferences for, and types of experience. Especially if you live in or near a city, evidence of diversity is all around you. If you go to college, any college, there is diversity everywhere. Sometimes you can see it right in front of you from the color of someone's skin, and sometimes you need to look deeper than the surface. But it is definitely there.

Christianity itself is rooted in diversity. God thought it best to create both females and males to capture the divine image in the world (Genesis 1:27). As the medieval philosopher Thomas Aquinas argued, "The presence of multiplicity and variety among created things was therefore necessary that a perfect likeness to God be found in them according to their manner of being."[12] In other words, diversity in creation better reflects the infinite nature of the divine than a single finite creature ever could.

In holding to the doctrine of the Trinity, Christians claim that God is diverse. There are three persons in the Godhead. Moreover, when God became human in the person of Jesus, he included the most diverse types of people in his call to prepare for the kingdom: fishermen (Peter, Andrew, James, and John), non-Jewish women (the woman at the well), political activists (Simon the Zealot), and even people of questionable morals (Judas Iscariot). There is also diversity within Christianity both because of the existence of different Christian denominations and because of different beliefs, worship, and practices within the same denomination.

Most important for our particular discussion here, however, is the issue of religious diversity with regard to our dating lives.

Given the diversity most of us live in, Christian or non-Christian, there is a chance that you just may fall in love with someone from a different tradition, whatever that may be. That special person might be Baptist, Methodist, or Catholic. He or she might even be Jewish, or Muslim, or Hindu. You never know who you are going to fall in love with.

As we said earlier, falling in love is both spiritual and mysterious. We also talked about how falling in love is truly a gift. It is also something that is difficult to control. Is falling in love with someone outside of your faith less of a gift?

Psychologist and religion scholar James Fowler describes faith as a "state of being ultimately concerned,"[13] and places faith at the foundation and center of our self-understanding. He contends that faith and spirituality are at the center, or core, of who we are, how we structure our lives and life journeys, and how we find meaning in the world. Through the expression and affirmation of our belief systems and values, we become who we are, define our identity, and struggle with changes and questions as we mature.

Yet if spirituality is central to who we are, what happens when we encounter someone whose core sense of self and meaning is different from our own? If faith is pivotal to our development, what effect does a relationship with someone of very distinct beliefs and values have on who we become in our relationship? Does it cause an identity crisis? Does it jeopardize our core? Do we have to sacrifice our faith in some way to make room for a different faith? Can the relationship work without one person sacrificing him- or herself to the other?

Dating someone different may cause us to question all of the above. For Fowler, though, an identity crisis or a rethinking of our core values and beliefs is not negative. As we have mentioned before, it is precisely this questioning and struggling that can be the source of our spiritual development. Fowler points out that encountering someone who is different from us and who does not automatically affirm what we already believe is often the stuff that helps enhance our faith and can enrich our understanding of self, beliefs, and God. Opening up to a faith different from our own helps us reflect on the role and structure of faith in our lives. It may sometimes move us to a more advanced stage of faith, according to Fowler.[14]

To be open to these possibilities requires that both people respect each other as persons and with regard to their individual life concerns and values. Respect does not require a couple to blindly accept everything each other says or insist that one person must always agree with the other. It does demand that both people take what the other thinks and believes seriously. Both should ponder, reflect, and discuss what each believes. Together you need to ask questions about what is true.

Respect is hard to achieve if one half of the couple is trying to convert the other half. Entering into a relationship motivated by a hope to convert someone — for that matter, entering into any relationship with the hopes of fundamentally changing the other person — is not wise. Not only would the person entering the relationship be trying to fix instead of love the other person, the relationship itself would be in tension with the diversity that God established.

Does this mean, then, that to grow in faith, you should, if you are a Christian, be looking to date a Buddhist?

Of course not. There are different ways to grow spiritually in our lives. However, opening up to someone different, even in terms of our religious beliefs and practices, is not inherently wrong. It can enhance our sense of spirituality in life. It can open us to discovering a new sense of meaning in our faith, it can challenge our faith, and it can assist us in discovering the incredible meaning possible through other types of faith traditions. Challenges to what we believe can turn out to be the richest spiritual resource we encounter.

What is required of us in the midst of diversity is that we struggle to understand and learn from each other. Sometimes this questioning and reflecting transforms us and sparks a change in our beliefs and values. But often it doesn't — and that is also

OK. When entering into an interfaith relationship, we must be aware that the possibilities of enrichment for both people from this relationship are great, and that it is also possible that faith differences may be the source of breaking up someday.

You never know unless you try though. We argue that it's OK to fall in love with someone of a different faith. You might be surprised by the spiritual growth possible in your life by dating someone with a faith different than your own.

You might even end up celebrating Easter *and* Passover — and celebrating Easter and Passover can be pretty nice. By celebrating both, you may find that they each end up enriching the experience of the other.

What more could you ask for?

An Evangelical and a Catholic Go Out on a Date

In graduate school, we both met Chris McMahon. Professors and students often knew him for his strong Catholic beliefs. To us, though, he was a good friend. Thus, we were both happy and sad when he got a job at Mt. Marty College in Yankton, South Dakota. Out there he quickly met and started to date Deb Phaser. She turned out to be quite an amazing woman. She was smart, cool, bilingual (Spanish and English), liked Chris (a big plus in our book), and was a committed Christian. It seemed like an ideal match.

And it was, except for one thing: Chris was Catholic (very), and Deb was evangelical Protestant (very). Both took their faith seriously and had good experiences within their traditions. It was a serious issue they faced while dating each other. (They have since married.) So, when we decided to write about interdenominational dating, we gave them a call to ask about their experience.

What follows is the conversation that I (Jason) had with them. What we had initially envisioned was taking what they had to say and putting it in our own words, but we thought it would be good to have some voices other than ours speak.

Phone Conversation

Jason: Thanks for agreeing to do this. What can you tell me about the struggles and joys of interdenominational dating?

Deb: Thanks for asking us. For us, the foundation of the relationship has been a shared commitment to Christianity. Each of our traditions gave us this love of the faith, and it was our good experiences in each tradition that enabled us to open up to each other. We felt happy and secure enough in our own communities to be open to something new. It was our strong commitments that enabled the dating to work. If one of us had not been interested in our faith, the relationship probably would not have worked.

Chris: Integrity does become an issue though. One's good experiences make one loyal to one's own tradition. Interdenominational dating demands a compromising of this tradition. The question is really when is the compromising also growing? And when is it a departure from the true self?

Deb: Integrity is a struggle. In the course of the relationship, I found myself publicly defending Chris and his Catholicism to my evangelical family and friends while I was privately struggling with the issue inside. The struggle was especially hard because my family was always very good to me and also responsible for giving me my faith. Thus, I felt pulled in my love for another, my own tradition, my family, and myself. I remember driving to Sioux Falls and wondering why I would pick someone from another tradition to date. All of our friends think we would be the last two people to ever date someone outside of our own tradition. My answer was that we were able to interact and challenge each other, and from this, we both grew tremendously. It was what made the relationship successful.

Chris: For me, the key to our success was that we were not only committed to a particular tradition but also to talking, studying, and arguing about God and faith. We were both committed to thinking theologically. This shared intellectual pursuit is what is central to our faith today and to the success of our dating. We are able to take each other seriously, yet argue and see the arguing as a fruitful enterprise.

Deb: Disagreement can be painful, but, because it challenges us, it is good. The questioning and the curiosity are good and really make things work. Also, at the heart of it is a deep respect for another person, really knowing that this person has a spiritual life, a spiritual life that is attractive, honest, and compelling. It is only because we respect the person that we are able to respect his or her tradition.

Chris: The only way it [an interdenominational relationship] can work is to build trust in a spiritual sense. This is not just being honest but really trusting another's character and faith to be crucial to one's own salvation. Without trust, I cannot see how you could date or why you would want to.

Jason: How do you develop spiritual trust?

Chris: It begins with something as simple as reciprocity in worship. It means overcoming fears of some other tradition, being able to talk about things that are different or that bother you and things that you like. Praying together is crucial. It helps you discuss images of God. Without that communication and shared experience, you cannot start building spiritual trust.

Deb: Spiritual trust also takes time. It may not even be a conscious act but merely showing curiosity, interest, or respect for the other's tradition. Also, meeting and getting to know people in the other's tradition whom you respect and are good Christian witnesses. In some sense, though, interdenominational dating is easier than marriage. Issues that are serious for marriage are not as serious if you are only dating.

Jason: Examples?

Chris: Baptism, church membership, birth control, education, kids, all of these are issues that come up in marriage and not in dating. Visiting each other's church is no big deal, but, when you are married, it is different. Can I be happy going to my wife's church all the time? Can I be a member of it? Can I participate in some real sense and still be a member of my own church?

Deb: To return to the topic, though, dating...

Chris: Are you accusing me of digressing?

Deb: Yes. [Background laughter.] Dating is a chance for exploring the good of the self and the good of the other. Dating is an intellectual opportunity.

Chris: Interdenominational dating has to be able to work in the abstract for the couple; otherwise it is frustrating and aggravating. People have to be able to imagine that another person can bring good to them. Dating can be amazingly enriching, impacting each other and each other's tradition in a good way. For us, it was only good and interesting because we were faithful to our own tradition and community.

Jason: You mentioned earlier that interdenominational dating was not as hard as marriage, but you did not say it was easy either. What are some of the difficulties you face?

Deb: What are the painful points? There is a surprising amount of sacrifice on both our parts. While we were dating, and even now that we are married, Chris does not go to communion because I cannot go. This is an amazing sacrifice on Chris's part, but I still feel alienated. It would be easier if we both had the same tradition.

Chris: Family relationships are also difficult. Deb's family is very united to her church experience, and her church has historically defined itself in opposition to Catholicism. Even though her parents were totally cool from the beginning, I was not quite prepared for the evangelical suspicion of Catholics. After I started dating Deb, her parents wanted to sit down with me and talk about my faith. Some of my other friends have had this experience of the parents wanting to talk. For them, it turned out to be a disaster. For me it turned out well. I thought it was totally appropriate. Still, going through the realization that they were suspicious of my faith was hard.

Deb: It was hard on me because choosing to be with Chris implied a sense of separation, a stepping away from my family. I also wanted feelings of security about the future, and it is hard to imagine a future within the context of such different faith traditions. All the things that you knew as a kid, all the things you thought would be there when you grew up, might not be there because the other person is different. Also, interdenominational dating is hard because you do not feel comfortable in another tradition. You think, "This is not me," "I do not want to be here," "This is dumb," "I don't understand this." You need to be able to work through these questions, work through the disillusionment.

You always feel like you are giving more than the other person. This is probably true in all relationships, but it is deeply challenging when there are denominational differences.

Jason: Having said all of this, what do you think the value of interdenominational dating is?

Chris: I have a quote from Pope John Paul II. It reads: "Marriages between Catholics and other baptized persons have their own particular nature, but they contain numerous elements that could well be made good use of and developed, both for their intrinsic value and for the contribution that they can make to the ecumenical movement. This is particularly true when both parties are faithful to their religious duties. Their common baptism and the dynamism of grace provide the spouses in these marriages with the basis and motivation for expressing their unity in the sphere of moral and spiritual values."[15] This is a great quote. I believe it summarizes our perspective. Interdenominational dating can have a significant impact in overcoming the misunderstandings between churches and work toward greater unity.

Thanks for sharing, Deb and Chris.

When a Woman Loves a Woman and a Man Loves a Man

Speaking of diversity, there is also diversity in sexual orientation. There are all types of sexual identities, from heterosexual to homosexual to bisexual to transsexual. There are LGBT (lesbian, gay, bisexual, transgender) open communities on most college campuses today, and offices where young people can safely struggle with their sexuality, find services if they want counseling, "come out" and celebrate their identity, as well as encounter an LGBT friendly, social community. Discussions about sexuality are no longer taboo, particularly at colleges and universities.

Today the likelihood is that you at least know someone, if not are friends with a person, who is *not* heterosexual. It is also possible that you may not know it because the person is not "out." Or you who are reading this may be lesbian, gay, bisexual, or transgendered, and are searching to understand how your identity is compatible with your spiritual life.

What's an LGBT person who is also a spiritual person to do?

The world's religious traditions have not gazed favorably on any sexual orientation outside of heterosexuality, and the Christian tradition is no exception. Given the fact that American culture and religion in general do not recognize same-sex relationships and marriages, or even the legitimacy of sexual orientations other than the heterosexual one, this issue is difficult to attend to. Christians have a tough time addressing and condoning heterosexual dating, much less LGBT dating.

The unfortunate reality of the complicated relationship between LGBT sexual orientations and religion makes it important for us to address it here. This essay gives us the opportunity to raise the topic and initiate some questions. Know up front that a few pages of discussion falls far short of what is necessary to tackle the topic of LGBT sexual orientations in relation to dating and spirituality — that would take an entire book, if not several.

However, we feel it essential to share a few thoughts with you.

Thought #1: *You do not have to be heterosexual to be a spiritual person.*

Sarah and Kate, two friends of ours, have an incredible relationship. They met, fell in love, and are deeply committed to each other. They work hard at their relationship, support each other emotionally and in their work, and walk together in life and in community. They are one of those couples you meet, spend some time with and realize they are meant to be together.

Both come from Christian backgrounds and by all counts are in what could be described as a very "Christian," loving and committed relationship — except for the fact that they are both lesbians, of course. They describe themselves as spiritual people, yet do not go to mass on Sundays or affiliate with any particular church. They find Christianity alienating because of their sexual identity. Associating themselves with the Christian faith became too difficult, so they eventually gave up trying.

As we have noted above as well as in other places in the book, sexuality in general is a difficult issue for Christians. The popular inclination for almost two thousand years of spiritual history has been more or less to forget that we are sexual beings altogether. The body is often denigrated within the Christian tradition as a "prison" for the soul, something that keeps us from the spiritual. Expressing human sexuality even within heterosexual marriage is a conversation topic often regarded as better not discussed.

With all this anxiety over sexuality in general and dating in particular, it is difficult to throw the issue of sexual identity into the mix on top of everything else. Yet, as we said earlier, you do not have to be a heterosexual person to be a spiritual person, or, to be dating. We find it unfortunate that couples like Sarah and Kate must either deny themselves the possibility of dating and longer term romantic relationships altogether, or leave the Christian faith. The preservation of one's identity as a spiritual person is difficult for someone who is not heterosexual, even if they disassociate religion and spirituality. It is even more difficult to develop the spiritual dimensions of an LGBT relationship within a faith tradition that does not support the existence of these relationships at all.

Thought #2: *Christians can no longer pretend that sexual diversity does not exist.*

Avoidance is not an option especially for the younger generations of Christians. We aren't our mothers and fathers. We grow up today in communities (especially in city communities) and on college campuses where sexual diversity is a part of life. We need to figure out what this means to us in terms of religion and spirituality.

By ignoring the issue, by not engaging someone in his or her full humanity, which includes sexuality, we participate in alienating particular groups from Christianity and ultimately from God.

Many scholars today define sin in terms of alienation or isolation from God. We can alienate ourselves from God by shutting ourselves off from a relationship with God by intellectual choice or through life decisions that turn us away from the divine. We can also be alienated from God via our social circumstances. Society can construct its norms so that we become alienated from understanding ourselves as valuable persons with respect to the divine. Religion can construct its norms so that we become alienated from the concept that we, too, are made in God's image. A common example within the Christian tradition of this is with regard to the role and stereotypes of women. Many women have left the Catholic Church because of a patriarchal hierarchy, patriarchal view of God, as well as its overall view of women, yet in their anger or disappointment in leaving the Church they also leave behind God. This experience of alienation also happens with regard to LGBT men and women. When religious communities participate in the isolation of persons and particular groups through social structures, they are guilty of social sin.

Of course, talking about sin and sexual orientation is a complicated issue — especially when we imply above that alienating the LGBT lifestyle from religion is sinful while at the same time much of Christianity labels the lifestyle as sinful itself. We realize this is no simple matter for practicing Christians — whether heterosexual or LGBT.

Yet we must reflect today on the unwillingness of many Christians to engage the issue of sexual identity in general and relationships, both dating and marital, in particular. We must also reflect on the fear of many Christians to even breach the topic of sexual orientation. By leaving LGBT people totally out of the Christian lifestyle, are we guilty of sin?

Thought #3: *The same possibilities for spiritual growth, personal and relational enrichment, and interpersonal and spiritual struggles exist for people of all sexual identities.*

Our concern throughout the book has been seeing dating relationships — whatever from they take — in light of spirituality and the Christian faith. Obviously we would like everyone to read this book and proclaim it great, perfect, and relevant to their sense of spirituality and faith life. This is unrealistic, of course. What we really hope is that you will take what we say seriously, evaluate it based on your own beliefs and experiences, and build on it. In other words, we hope to challenge you, whether you are a believer or nonbeliever, spiritual-but-not-religious, Catholic or Protestant, hetero-/homo-/bi-/transsexual. People of all sexual identities can take up the issues we have raised here because anybody can be a spiritual person *and* a Christian.

And if the Sarahs and Kates of the world do read this book, we hope they can find material that is not only good and helpful but also challenging. This would be true inclusiveness.

So what do we think about the relationship between spirituality and LGBT dating? Regardless of our sexual orientation, we are embodied persons, made in the image of God, with the capacity to express our love for each other in a multitude of ways. Thus, there is as great personal and spiritual potential in LGBT relationships as there is in heterosexual dating. The differences lies in the social and religious challenges LGBT couples must face in addition.

Last thought: *We know what some of you are thinking.*

We know that some of you who are Christian and reading this are thinking the Bible says that any sexual orientation outside of the heterosexual one is wrong and sinful. We know this because lots of our readers have stumbled over this issue when they got to it in our book.

Biblical quotations taken out of context and apart from the interpretive lens of tradition and community experience can be used to say a lot of things. The Bible historically was used to justify and oppose slavery here in the United States. The Bible has been used for both the liberation of people as well as the perpetuation of their oppression. The Bible can be used to say many things, both good and bad. Christians today look back on how the Bible was used by some to justify slavery in dismay and sorrow. Will Christians look back on the topic of sexual orientation in the same way some day too?

On a final note, in reflecting on this topic we should call to mind the people Jesus chose to hang out with during his lifetime. How do we think Jesus would have interacted with people of different sexual orientations?

Some food for thought.

Dating Is Not All Roses and Chocolates

For most of the book, we have talked about the spiritual value and benefits of dating, but as most of us know, dating also has its challenges and pains. This section (and the next one as well) seeks to recognize these difficulties and, in some cases, turn them into new possibilities. Thus, dating often "shipwrecks" us by forcing us to realize, painfully at times, who we genuinely are and who we want to be. Our past actions, ones we are proud of and ones we are not so happy about, can be opportunities for growth as long as we do not ignore them or bury them. In our relationships, it is important to recognize that infatuation is not love, though sometimes we mistake the two. The loneliness we experience as a result of a breakup is very difficult as well, but we must try not to let loneliness be our sole motive for dating. Love, not fear, should move us.

There's one last thing about this section that I (Jason) want to point out to readers. While the first two essays may not have the scripture quotes that many desire, I believe that the idea they address—bringing good out of difficulties or reevaluations of different experiences—is at root Christian. Because God has chosen to respect our freedom, God cannot stop sin, but God can and does bring good out of evil (see Romans 6 and 11). The death of Jesus was not a good thing, but God turned his death into life for all.

Thus, as God turns our failures or misfortunes into opportunities for grace, so we should work to do the same.

Dating Shipwrecks Us

 We grow up thinking of ourselves as "selves" — concrete, tangible, and explainable objects. Somewhere along the line our sense of self eventually begins to shift. Sometimes this occurs during a college psychology or philosophy class when we are told we are not really what we always thought we were. Thanks to the philosophers and psychologists today, we learn that the self is a bit more "slippery" or difficult to pin down than we thought. Other times, we realize that the seemingly obvious identity we carried with us to college as "star football player," "student government president," or "math geek" (i.e., Jason) is not so obvious anymore. It seems that our "self" turns into something more than what we thought it was. The math geek discovers he can go out with the hot soccer player, and the star football player learns he has an unexpected affinity for art history.

As we grow beyond high school, we experience changes in our sense of self. We realize we are not who we thought we were, we are not who we would like to be, or even that we have no idea who we are or who we want to be. Our "selves" are thrown into crisis. Some of us experience crises on a very small scale and others in a life-changing way.

Sharon Parks, author of *Big Questions, Worthy Dreams: Mentoring Young Adults in Their Search for Meaning*, identifies the "dissolution" of self and the life altering possibilities of crisis as resources for meaningful growth. It is through our crises, our transformations, our "dissolutions," often sparked by something we've read, a person we have met, or a professor who has challenged our thinking, that we begin the process of rebuilding our sense of who we are and how we perceive our "selves." Parks refers to these crises of self as "shipwrecks," and it is life's "shipwrecks" that are often the spark of spiritual growth.[16]

Throughout the history of Christian spirituality, there have been many spiritual shipwrecks. These shipwrecks, or changes of the heart, led individuals like St. Augustine to become Christian, St. Francis to give up all his possessions and work and live among the poor, Martin Luther to redefine what Christianity means to the world, Dorothy Day to leave her partner Forster, and Malcolm X to move from criminal to spiritual leader. While these examples may be more extreme than the everyday spiritual shipwrecks of life — which may include anything from realizing the need to switch majors to telling a friend you are upset with her — they are no less significant. Like the experience of falling in love that teaches us about spiritual shifting (falling in love with God or becoming concerned with ultimate meaning), changes in understanding our "self" and changes of the heart can be the stuff of spiritual shipwrecks.

And of course, dating can be the source of these shipwrecks of self as well.

We have talked about understanding dating as a spiritual journey, as a potential source of spiritual transformation, as a teacher of spiritual intimacy. Thus far we have mainly portrayed the beauty, joy, and excitement that can arise from dating relationships in our lives. Yet as with any journey, transformation, or learning experience, one must expect changes and challenges to our sense of who we are along the way. Dating relationships change us and this changing can be difficult and sometimes painful.

Shipwrecks don't often feel like vacations, but that does not make them any less valuable.

The intimacy called for in a dating relationship that is committed, if only for a finite period, requires a certain amount of making yourself vulnerable to another person. Whenever we make ourselves vulnerable to another person, we become open to new possibilities, new ideas, new ways of understanding our "selves." We also open ourselves to being hurt.

One of the challenges of making ourselves vulnerable to each other is what this vulnerability allows us to see in ourselves. Often it's as if someone handed us a mirror, allowing us to see ourselves in a way we've never seen before. Sometimes, what we see of ourselves in the mirror has a rosy glow — we find ourselves beautiful, fun, and intelligent — things that we can see through the help of the other person. At others, we are shown aspects of ourselves we wish we had been protected from seeing — we find ourselves jealous, deceitful, unable to communicate.

Understanding relationships as having a "mirroring" effect on how we see ourselves is a focus of contemporary, relational psychology. For Heinz Kohut, a German psychoanalyst, our relationships with others are at the foundation of our self-development. Beginning with our parents, other people become mirrors for us from the earliest moments of life. Our experiences seeing ourselves in those around us can be the source of a strong and healthy sense of who we are, or one that is fragile, as if we see ourselves in a mirror that is shattered. These experiences can even reveal an aspect of ourselves in the mirror that we did not know existed. We realize we can act in ways we didn't know we were capable of acting, both good and bad.

The "mirroring" effect of others on our sense of self is obviously powerful and may seem intimidating. The idea that our mirrors can become broken, resulting in a distortion of our sense of self, or that they can reveal something darker inside of us that we did not know was there, sounds frightening. It means that other people, if we make ourselves vulnerable to them, can hurt our self-esteem, damage a once-positive view of ourselves, or encourage us to be someone we do not really want to be.

Though it is always possible that those we date can have a negative impact on our sense of self and our spiritual journeys, running from relationships because of this possibility does not make sense. If we accept the idea that we are relational beings — we cultivate relationships with parents, friends, partners, and God throughout our lives — then we should not turn away from a dating relationship because it might show us things about ourselves we don't want to see. Any relationship can awaken us to painful self-realizations or turn us to activities in which we are better off not engaging. There is no doubt that our relationships with others can impact us in difficult and negative ways — yet all relationships can do this, not just dating ones. Friendships and even parental relationships can have a powerful impact. It is in the nature of relationships, be they with friends, relatives, or dates, to be the causes of life's shipwrecks.

Dating relationships, however, can make us particularly susceptible to life's shipwrecks because they usually require an intense level of intimacy and also usually end at some point. We pay more attention to the mirrors that our dating relationships hold up to us because they are frequently so central to our lives, if only temporarily. The mirrors of ourselves we see through dating may awaken us to painful images — self-aspects we try to keep hidden — both from others and ourselves. Dating relationships are perhaps quicker to show us things about ourselves that are difficult to look at, and more likely to leave us to face these things alone.

Nevertheless, these mirrors also help us to see the good in ourselves and how we can become better people. In helping us to see, they also help make us more spiritually and ethically sound, strengthen our resolve to do what is right, and lead us toward new paths we had never before considered. In dating, the mirrors held up to us help in constructing our spiritual journeys. All spiritual journeys include shipwrecks — times of crises and changes of the heart, both big and small.

Changes of the heart are often painful, but pain is not a reason to avoid dating. Changes of the heart are essential to spiritual growth, growth in ourselves as relational beings, as loving persons, as lovers of God. While some relationships can withstand this kind of transformation, others cannot. Either way, these "shipwrecks" are critical to spiritual development. They can be the stuff that sparks the beginnings and turning points of our spiritual journeys.

Eventually we always heal — even if only to find ourselves shipwrecked once again. As Sharon Parks tells her readers, it is often in the shipwrecks of our lives that we discover life's most meaningful places.

Perhaps following the shipwreck, we will find ourselves on a beautiful beach.

So You're a Born-Again Virgin

 So you have had a lot of sex. Or maybe not so much. Just some. You've had a little bit of sex. Maybe even just once. If you're somewhere on this spectrum, then you're not a virgin. Virginity is something that, once lost, you can never get back. Or can you?

A friend of ours, now single, had a very healthy, very long-term relationship for about four years. The person she dated was her first sexual partner. They cultivated a very loving, fulfilling sexual dimension in their relationship, but decided not to make a lifelong commitment to each other.

After breaking up, our friend went out and had a few one-night stands with guys she didn't know very well. She also had a few short-term relationships that included a sexual element. None of these was as fulfilling as her first experience in the long-term relationship.

One day she decided, "No more until I get married. I am done with sex until then."

Today there is a new category of virginity emerging that includes our friend: the "renewed virgins" or the "secondary abstinents."

The *born-again virgins.*

This new group of virgins is everywhere. A born-again virgin is someone who has had sex at least once if not many times, but has made the decision not to have any more sex until marriage or until she or he finds a lifelong partnership. Born-again virgins range in age from the teens into the thirties and even the forties. Most often we find them in the twenty-something or very early thirty-something age range.

Why would anyone choose to make this decision? Is it real? Are those who claim born-again virginity kidding themselves into feeling better about past experiences?

It is no secret that single people today have a wide range of sexual experiences. More often than not, young people have had sex at least once. By the teen years, many people choose to have sex. Many think this decision is normal. Others think it is problematic or sinful.

We believe that sexual experiences, whatever they may be or have been, should not be buried in a dark corner of your memory. You may decide that yes, a past experience was a mistake, and indeed it may have been. But you cannot wish past experiences away. You can pretend that they never happened. Or you can engage those experiences as a mature, reflective person who wants to understand the significance of your past experiences and learn from them because they are a part of who you are. Burying them or trying to wish them away is never the healthiest approach because our past allows us to make present-day choices. Without the past, we would not have the same information to make the decisions we do today.

No matter what you do, your past is a part of who you are.

This valuing of the past is where we believe the born-again virginity category comes in. For people to declare themselves a born-again, somewhere, somehow, they have come to the conclusion that having sex in their dating relationships is not working or has not worked in the past. They may have decided that sex is not as satisfying as they thought it might be. Or perhaps their personal or spiritual self-understanding has taken a turn, calling them to let go of this dimension of their relationships, at least for now. Or they may have decided that, despite experiencing a loving, healthy, sexual relationship outside of marriage, there is a difference between having sex with someone you love, at least for now, and having sex with someone you've made a commitment to for the rest of your life.

The only way a person can come to any of the conclusions above is by way of their past experiences. You don't have to have sex, of course, to decide that you would prefer to wait and have it with your lifelong partner. Yet for some people, it is only by having past experiences that they gain this knowledge and make this type of decision.

Our experiences affect our spiritual journey. Engaging in sex outside of marriage doesn't have to alienate you from your faith; it simply may mean that your spiritual journey is different from someone who decides not to have sex. To understand it in this way, however, means that you must do the work required in reflecting on and understanding our actions and choices. Upon doing this work, you may just decide that born-again virginity is for you.

Are born-again virgins just pretending?

If those in this category use the title to deny their past, then yes.

We think that born-again virginity implies something different though. We think born-again virginity says a lot about young people and sex today, and much of it is positive. Declaring one-self a born-again implies that a person acknowledges that he or she has a sexual past. It suggests that a person has thought intensely about the significance of sexual experiences in relation to who he or she is not and who he or she hopes to become. It indicates a willingness to make changes on one's life journey, changes that involve a new view of sexuality in relationships — a view not easily maintained today. Finally, as we noted above, deciding to become a born-again involves a choice that can only be made through experience — it is made because one has a sexual past. Without the past, one could not then form this renewed perspective on sexuality. It implies a deepened understanding of sexuality and its role in both dating and lifelong relationships.

While born-again virginity may not be for everyone, we believe that it can be an empowering way to incorporate one's sexual past into one's relationship future. It does not require one to bury past experience. It encourages one to evaluate where one has been to assist in where one will go as one continues to date. Born-again virginity supports personal and relational responsibility with regard to sex.

Taking responsibility for the past, present, and future is a good thing.

How Infatuation Differs from Love

DANCING

Almost all of us have known people who are infatuated with each other. We may have even been infatuated with someone once or twice ourselves. Infatuated people talk about and are with each other all the time. They want to be with each other more than anything else. They sometimes call each other cutesy names or whisper to each other even when they are with their friends.

150

You know the people. They can be sickening (unless you are one of them).

Infatuation, however, does not just happen between people. I (Jason) have watched this infatuation happen among friends and acquaintances, of all places, in soccer. Although I played soccer throughout high school and college and still today I play in some recreational leagues, I am not infatuated with the sport. I know this to be true because I have played with people who are. They are the forty- and fifty-year-old men whose whole life is absorbed in soccer. They, in the deep sense of the term, love it. They play on several different teams at once. On occasion, they skip work to play in a game. They hang out after their own game to watch other games. They get cable solely to watch the sport on TV. When you talk to them, they almost exclusively talk about the sport: "Remember that game between Argentina and Germany in 1972?" You can barely participate in the conversation because you do not know these esoteric references to past games. People infatuated with soccer turn out to be more like an encyclopedia of soccer than human beings.

Weird.

The extreme soccer players described above are similar to infatuated couples. Both types are totally immersed in their own interest. They both see everything else as less important. The primary difference between them lies in the fact that the soccer players discussed have been infatuated for years while the couples are usually only infatuated at the beginning of the relationship.

The infatuated soccer player provides us with a glimpse of what happens to people when infatuation goes unchecked. People become unreasonably attached to the object of their affection. They not only think about it all the time but also do not think about anything else. The world becomes defined only by those issues related to their infatuation. In short, they become narrow people, finding it difficult to maintain any other relationships or interests. Either willfully or through ignorance, they put everything else in life below what infatuates them. The diverse joys of the world are lost.

When this extreme is applied to a dating relationship, infatuation can lead to the devaluing of everything except for the person one desires. The phrase "all is fair in love and war" has some validity for them. Goodness, truth, and beauty all become secondary issues. All one cares about and thinks about is the object of one's affection.

C. S. Lewis warned of this narrowing in his allegory *The Great Divorce*. The book is about a spiritual journey from hell to purgatory. Once in purgatory, the souls have a chance of reaching heaven. This journey is made in, of all things, a bus. The people in hell must get on a bus that transports them to purgatory if they hope to eventually end up in heaven. Not a bad deal.

It seems rather easy to get to heaven, yet people still decide not to board the bus and choose to remain in hell.

The protagonist in Lewis's story lines up for the bus trip to heaven. While waiting in line, he encounters two couples. The first is in front of him in line, but they leave because of a fight. The man of the couple follows the woman apologetically by saying, "I have only been trying to please *you*, for peace sake. My own feelings are of course a matter of no importance."[17] The other couple behind the main character ends up leaving the line as well. They pass him "arm and arm ... [and] ... it was clear that each for the moment preferred the other to the chance of a place in the bus."[18] Each of the two couples are so absorbed in each other and their relationship that they fail to see the significance of what lies ahead of them if they get on the bus to heaven.

These couples provide a good example of the problems with infatuation. They both place another person in front of everything and everyone else. The hope of greater joy, truth, and love —

what Christians call heaven — is sacrificed because the people are too absorbed in each other to notice their opportunity for it. Relationships based on infatuation are narrow, admit of no greater possibility than the confines of the couple, and are lacking the riches of life's fullness that involves openness beyond the relationship to a wider community.

We all know people like the couples described above. They are the couples who drop off the face of the earth once they find each other, neglecting friendships, social interaction outside of their relationship, and any obligations that may take them away from each other. Their interest in each other often borders on obsession, and they act possessively of each other's time and attention to a level that is unhealthy. They are also the people who, when the infatuation wanes, find themselves in hot water with their friends when suddenly they want to hang out again.

Obviously the narrow vision that infatuation causes us is different than love. Love causes us to desire and do what is good for another person on many different levels, including those things that may take our beloved away from us if they are to the benefit of the person we love. Love opens us to a wider world that includes the self, lover, family, friends, neighbors, strangers, enemies, and God. Love expands our vision and ourselves, and what is possible for us in the relationship. In love, we not only see the beloved, but we also are able to expand and transform our understanding of the world in light of this love.

A good example of this expanding element of love is found in the movie *City of Angels* starring Nicholas Cage and Meg Ryan. In the movie, Nicholas Cage portrays one of many angels that watch and listen to people. They take notes about what they observe and talk to each other about it. Cage's character, Seth, however, falls in love with Maggie, Meg Ryan's character. This love draws Seth from his existence as an angel to existence as a human. He meets Maggie and starts to experience all of the new and exciting things of this world, including a relationship. His love, far from narrowing his existence, expands his world greatly, and in ways he could not have imagined.

It is love that expands and enhances our vision that we are called to express in the context of our spiritual journeys. The experience of being loved and loving another should not lead us only to see love in the other person we are loving. Ideally the experience of giving and receiving love should make us overflow with a love that incorporates others, be they friends, family, or strangers we encounter in the streets. The liberation spiritualities and theologies of Dorothee Soelle, bell hooks, and Gustavo Gutiérrez claim that the experience of love should ultimately translate into a desire for love, justice, and healing for all people. This understanding of life finds its root in Jesus. He continually practiced a love that overflowed into a concern for all others. He opened the eyes of the blind, both physically and spiritually, healed the sick, and cured the lame. As a result of these loving actions, these people were able to grow in their understanding of the world. They were no longer hindered from moving on to other interests and concerns or socializing with others. They were able to experience life more fully. Christians are called to practice love that builds people up instead of restricts them.

This is the kind of love that should permeate our whole existence, including the love we practice in our dating relationships. The kind of love we ultimately need in a romantic relationship is the kind that expands us. It is a kind of love that moves us to see the world in a new way, a way that is more attentive to what is genuinely beautiful and truly good.

Granted, our experiences of love and infatuation, especially at the beginning of a relationship, can be very similar. They both involve strong feelings that extend to another person. But infatuation prevents the person from going beyond these initial feelings. A love that restricts us in our abilities to love others or do what is right should not be mistaken for the love we are talking about here. If you believe in the expansive nature of love, then the self-ish characteristics that arise in us through infatuation should be a warning sign to either end an unhealthy relationship or work to change it. Love points to a world that encompasses but goes beyond the initial giddiness of infatuation and is a sign of a healthy dating relationship.

So, despite the similar feelings, there is a crucial difference between infatuation and love. The best way to capture the difference is to use a metaphor. Imagine yourself enjoying the house where you live. It is comfortable, has all your possessions, and everything you need. Infatuation would keep you from leaving the house. You would insist that the house is the highest good and that nothing else beyond the house would be better.

Love, on the other hand, would insist that the house is still good and that you still need to enjoy it, but love would demand that you leave it once in a while. It would move you to visit other houses of friends and family. You can then return to your own house, knowing that it is only one instance, albeit a very vivid and special one, of the good that is present throughout the world.

Scared to Be Alone

 In graduate school, a friend of ours, Fred, was in the midst of a long dry spell. He had not been out on a date in several years. (We won't mention how long to keep from embarrassing him.) One day, a girl started pursuing him. While all of us, his friends, wanted him to have a date, we did not want him to date *her*. He was friendly, easygoing, and an all-around cool guy. We did not think she was a very good person nor did we trust her interest in Fred. We worried. After so long without a date, how could he resist? Even if she was not good for him, how could he continue to be alone?

Against all odds, Fred held out. He continued to hang out with us and worked on his degree. And, as it happens, a year later he met Lynda, the woman that eventually became his wife.

It sounds like a happy story, right? Well, it is except that being alone for several years is difficult. There are those Friday nights when all you really want to do is go out and have a fun, romantic evening, and those rainy days when it is so easy to feel sad. And, of course, there are those wonderful days of spring when suddenly the flowers are blooming, the birds are chirping, everyone seems to be in love and excited about someone, and you are by yourself.

Even the Garden of Eden is not so perfect when one is alone. Adam was alone before Eve, and God saw this and proclaimed it "not good" (Genesis 2:18). And this is the same God that spent seven days proclaiming everything — sun, moon, animals, plants, people, stars, water, land — "good" (Genesis 1:1–2:4).

What is the solution to the terror of loneliness?

One approach, the approach Fred did not take, is to date whoever comes along. Many of us have taken this route at one time or another. We get involved in a relationship even though we don't really want to be in it, or we remain in a relationship that we know is unhealthy because we fear being alone.

We may have even give the person we recently broke up with another chance because he or she made us laugh one night and were willing to walk us home later. We give them another chance because the alternative is to end up walking home alone.

Our dating relationships, even the awful ones, seem to protect us from that unhappy state of loneliness. There is something about having someone who is particularly and intensely focused on us, in a way different than our other, non-dating relationships. Dating someone give us that one-on-one companionship that we desire so profoundly during life's difficult moments as well as those times that would simply be more fun with someone else. When we date someone, he or she often makes us feel special and wanted in a way that a friendship does not. We occasionally seek this type of companionship just to have it; we even seek it with people we know in our hearts are not right for us nor are we right for them. Knowing in our hearts that we are probably better off ending a relationship or not getting involved in the first place does not make being alone any easier either.

So, if dating the first person that comes along is not always advisable, is the other option to just sit and wait for our Miss or Mr. Right to show up? No. "Unsuccessful dating" is often a learning experience. At the least, a bad date can make for amusing conversation with friends after the fact. Or sometimes people that seem wrong for us may in fact turn out to be just short of perfect for our future lives. Giving new and different people a try can be a good thing to do — that's how we end up unbelievably happy with people we never even dreamed of initially.

The problem with dating someone different occurs when we say yes to someone again and again, even when we know deep down that the person, the relationship, maybe even the timing is just wrong for us, or perhaps their companionship is unhealthy for our life on some level. We should not continue dating because the alternative — being alone again or remaining alone — is too scary an option.

If and when we feel lonely, we have choices to make about how to solve this problem. Those choices should be made neither haphazardly (i.e., date anyone) nor too conservatively (i.e., date no one). This, of course, is not an easy judgment to make, especially when we are longing to be that special someone for someone else.

Dorothy Day, the famous Catholic pacifist, journalist, and laborer for the poor, offers us a compelling vision of how to manage not being romantically involved. She struggled her whole life with a sense of loneliness, even titling her autobiography *The Long Loneliness*. She wanted companionship and sought it in a myriad of different ways. Some ways were good, others less so.

Her solution to this loneliness came after a radical youth, a common-law marriage, and years of community living with the Catholic Worker movement: "We have all known the long loneliness and we have learned that the only solution is love and that love comes with community."[19] Not being in a romantic relationship turned out to be the right option for her own life journey, a difficult decision to make for anyone.

Being alone or choosing to become alone is never easy, nor is it a state that most of us desire to be in for very long periods of time. Sometimes we have no choice, though, but to be alone. On the other end of the spectrum, we should not choose to remain in a relationship because we are afraid to be by ourselves either.

Instead we can turn to those that we love and that love us when we are not romantically involved. We can live and interact in a community of people that supports us. We can turn to our friends and family when romantic love has disappeared or is unavailable. While our friends and family are not a substitute for romantic love, the love we give and receive from friends and family fulfills us in other important and sustaining ways.

We can also turn to God in prayer. God's love keeps us company, especially through lonely times. Dorothy Day adds to this idea by saying, "We cannot love God unless we love each other, and to love we must know each other."[20] Thus, God can keep us company in the silence of prayer and through the love of the community.

Day's solution is to realize that ultimately, regardless of whether we are romantically or not romantically involved, we are never alone. Most of us have friends and family that love us, and God calls us to rely on them in times of need. Even if friends are in short supply, we are called to remember God's love for us, a love that does not fail.

One last thought about being alone: Remaining alone or becoming alone after a long time in a relationship requires an enormous amount of trust. You must trust in yourself — that you can weather the loneliness when you feel it and that life can be beautiful too, even when you are not in love. You must trust in your friendships — that though life may seem lonely on that Friday night, that there is love in your life all around you, just a different kind of love than what we find from that wonderful date we all hope to have.

And you must trust in the love of God in your life. If you truly have opened yourself to spirituality in your dating life, the loving dimension that is cultivated permeates all your experiences of love, be they love of self or love of friends.

In our times of dating aloneness, we must allow for that experience of spiritual love to reach us through other means. That spiritual love will help us make it through those times when we are tempted to continue a relationship with someone when we really should not, or say yes to a date when it is really better to say no.

It's OK to feel lonely sometimes. It's a part of life.

Trust that things will turn out well. Dorothy Day went through a long loneliness and found a solution in her community. Fred did not jump into the first relationship that came along just because he had been alone for a while. He waited. When we're lonely and long for a companion, it's important to take care and not let fear move us. We must have faith in ourselves, others, and in the spiritual ground on which we walk. Someday we may find someone to date, or someone to marry, or maybe even a totally new life pursuit.

Closing Doors, Opening Windows

The last section discussed how to respond to the pain we sometimes face in dating relationships. Here, we address what is often understood as the most painful aspect of dating: breaking up. We begin by pointing out that breaking up is not a failure. Sometimes people turn out to be too different or they change over the course of the relationship. Through no one's fault, the relationship does not work out. What then? We do not need to believe we have done something wrong when a relationship ends. We do, however, need to grow from it, and growing spiritually from our pain is possible. The only way to eliminate pain is to eliminate love too. Since God calls us to love, we cannot avoid pain. We must instead be open to its possibility so that we can love. Do not misunderstand us though. Pain is not fun or easy. It can seriously affect our attitude toward the world and dating. The effects of pain are why beginning again requires faith. We must take leaps of faith in order to work through our pain and experience new and greater joy. If we are Christian, we have to make this leap of faith. We have to love and practice loving and this is why loving matters in dating.

Breaking Up Is Not a Failure

I (Jason) remember very clearly the last day of third grade. The trees were green, the air was warm, and my backpack was heavy with all the school supplies I was lugging home. I was sitting in the back of the bus waiting for my stop, which, of course, was the last one on the route. The whole summer was spread out before me with no end in sight. I remember this day so well because of the shock I received in August.

I had to go back to school! My summer had gone quickly, and I could hardly remember what I had been doing the whole time. And now I had to return to desks and studies? How could my "summer without end" have ended?

While you may not have become sad over returning to school (though most of us probably did at some point in our lives), we would wager that you've experienced sadness over a great party or conversation or even dinner coming to end. The doldrums of the end naturally follow the enjoyment of the activity.

This sadness is often worse in dating relationships. We reflect on what went wrong, why it did so, and what could have been done differently. Sometimes we feel the whole process is a failure. We feel like we were not a good person, did not love well, or even dated a person that was totally wrong for us. We might even feel like we hurt another person. We feel guilty, and guilt is often a sign of sinful behavior.

This struggle after a breakup happened with both of us. Donna dated Jon. Jason dated Kimmery. Jon was a good guy. He was always honest, did not hold grudges, and worked hard. Kimmery was smart, driven, and fun. Everybody genuinely loved everybody else and sought, as best they could, to do what was good for the person they were dating. Still, the relationships did not work out. There were fights, disagreements, and eventually breakups. At the time, the two of us (Donna and Jason) sat around talking about what went wrong. Why did we fail in these relationships?

We bounced ideas off of each other: "Maybe there is something wrong with me and that is why this is not working out." "Maybe there is something wrong with them." "Perhaps we were not mature enough." "What if we had worked a little harder at the relationship?"

Both of us had experienced success in other aspects of our lives — school and jobs for example — so we struggled with the failure of these relationships. What did it say about who we are?

Often the feelings of failure that go along with a breakup lead people to crave the permanence of marriage. We look longingly at marriage as the relationship that never has to end. It involves the prince and the princess who finally find each other and acknowledge openly that they belong together. Marriage conjures up visions of wonderful romance and living "happily ever after." On a more practical level, marriage promises (or seems to at least) a long-term security in a relationship. If you are a religious person, you also believe that marriage is a particularly special union in the eyes of God.

Permanence, the infinite, and forever are qualities that we link to God. Since we are called to be like God, marriage, because it is forever, seems more in line with God's design than the temporary nature of dating. Breaking up, then, means moving away from the divine, away from salvation, right?

If we think about it, though, even marriage itself is not permanent. Jesus himself said that after we die, we "neither marry nor are given in marriage" (Luke 20:35). During wedding ceremonies the line "till death do us part" is usually spoken by each member of the couple. Further, in today's culture we all know that though marriages start with the intention of lasting throughout our lives, the failure rate of marriages is high.

We are finite creatures. We are born, live, and die. All of our activities are left incomplete. Even those who we often consider saints in the modern world, people like Mother Teresa and Martin Luther King Jr., had to pass on the work to their followers. They could not complete it in their own lifetime.

A few Christians claim that this finitude and death stems from original sin. From the book of Genesis, they argue that mortality, the finite nature of what it means to be human, came as a result of

Adam and Eve's disobedience. After Adam and Eve ate of the tree of the knowledge of good and evil, God banished them from the garden. Humans experience pain, suffering, sadness, and death as a consequence.

To rectify the consequences of the fall, Jesus is said to save humanity from this suffering. On the surface, though, it seems a very peculiar type of salvation. People still suffer. People still die. So what happened to salvation? We still seem to be trapped in our finitude. The permanence we seek is elusive.

Ultimately this interpretation of Christianity is not very Christian. The problem lies in understanding "to save" as "to escape." It depicts humanity as seeking a savior to help us avoid our problems instead of facing the consequences and taking responsibility for our choices.

For Christians, "to save" should mean something more like "to overcome," "to liberate," or as philosopher of religion Grace Jantzen tells us, "to flourish."[21] We do not overcome problems by avoiding them but instead by facing them. Jesus saves us not by providing an escape hatch from this world but by helping us to pick up our crosses and follow him. Salvation cannot avoid facing the cross.

Thus, we are saved not by avoiding our finitude, but by being raised up or "flourishing" in the face of our finitude. Writer Dorothy Sayers described the human condition well when she said that, too often, "our efforts are not directed, like those of the saint or the poet, to make something creative out of the idea of death, but rather to seeing whether we cannot somehow evade, abolish, and, in fact, solve the problem of death."[22]

As humans, we often learn to value that which seems more permanent over that which is less so. We believe that it is this type of belief that leads many Christian writers (like Joshua Harris) to devalue dating altogether, proclaiming it an obstacle to salvation.

Yet Sayers claims that our salvation comes not despite our finitude but *through it*.

Facing and experiencing endings is part of our humanity, part of our finitude.

We started this essay talking about breaking up and then end up discussing the flourishing of humanity. Trust us — the two points do connect! Just as we can experience salvation through our finitude, so, too, we can experience salvation and flourishing through the finitude of dating relationships. We need not flee these finite relationships as if they reflected the sins of Adam and Eve. Our salvation is not about "escaping" these relationships.

We can embrace dating and breaking up as a means of salvation — as part of our path toward flourishing in the light of God. If salvation is indeed *not* about being rescued, if it is *not* about someone else doing all the struggling on our behalf — if it instead requires our participation, reflection, creativity, and openness to God's presence in our lives, and willingness to struggle with it all — then we can begin to see salvation in light of who we are, what we do, and what we work through as humans who face finitude as an everyday part of life. Through dating relationships, however finite, we can come to a deeper understanding of what is truly valuable in our lives. We can become stronger in standing up for what we believe. We can learn to forgive others and ourselves.

Thus, the fact that relationships end is not sinful. Our experiences in breaking up provide a path toward salvation.

Breaking up is only a failure if we do not grow from it and if we do not do "something creative" with it. Wallowing in guilt, forgetting the whole process, or rejecting dating as sinful — these responses limit our cooperation with God.

In reflecting back on Jon and Kimmery, we both realized through our conversations that we had not "failed" in these relationships. We had not done something wrong. The relationships, through no one's fault, had not worked out.

It was a hard conclusion to accept. Yet it gave us freedom. We did not feel guilty nor did we try to blame Jon or Kimmery. Instead, we could reflect on the relationships and learn from them. The experiences challenged (and still challenge) us to improve our own lives and the way we relate with others. We would not trade those relationships for the world. They are part of who we are. They are part of our capacity to flourish as human beings today regardless of our finitude.

Despite the pain and difficulty, breaking up was not a failure.

Growing Spiritually from Our Pain

 We've talked about breaking up and said that it is spiritually valuable and that it even contributes to Christian salvation. Yet we never said it wouldn't hurt. In the children's fantasy book *The Giver* by Lois Lowry, there is no hurt or pain for anyone at all. There is no suffering, physical or emotional. There is no sadness. There is only life marching on in its routine way.

Those who inhabit this world that Lowry introduces to us are not exactly happy though. They are not sad either. They are just kind of there, living their lives, doing what they are told by the elders who run their community. They, like everyone else in the community, follow strict rules in order to maintain a life free of suffering.

Through following these rules, members of the community have no real concerns or problems, which seems nice — at least in the beginning. No one ever has to worry about finding a mate in life, because once they reach a certain age, they are given one. There are pills to be taken that ease all physical pains, no matter how serious. Tears from scraped knees are never shed. There is even a pill to remove all sexual desire, so no one ever has to be bothered by that kind of nuisance and what we know can be a dangerous area of potential heartache. No one ever experiences physical love — each couple is handed their children, always two and never more, at a special ceremony. They have people in the community assigned the roles of "birth mothers" to take care of the birthing (by artificial insemination, the reader is left to assume).

Each year in a child's life, from one until eleven (they all share the same birthday), a new milestone is celebrated by all the community. One year, the girls receive their hair ribbons; at nine all children in the community receive their bicycles (which is an especially exciting time for the children). Every designated birthday marks a special change in a child's life.

The age that everyone waits for, though, is the age of twelve. At twelve, the community assigns what is valued as most important in a person's life: the person's occupation. It is with this occupation that a child begins to serve the community for the rest of his or her life. A lot depends on the "celebration of the twelves."

It is one particular celebration of twelve that Lowry lets us in on. It is the celebration where a boy named Jonah receives the most important occupation of all, that of "Receiver" for his community. He, his family, and community all around him are shocked. A new Receiver is named maybe only once every twenty or thirty years. It is the highest honor of the community to receive this occupation.

No one knows what the Receiver does though — no one, that is, except for the Giver.

Jonah soon finds out what his new and mysterious occupation entails. Through the relationship he builds with the Giver, now a very old man, he learns that it is his occupation to "receive" and to bear all the world's memory on behalf of his community. He is to receive memories and experiences of extreme joy, which no one in the community knows of. Inevitably he is also to receive experiences of suffering too. Jonah quickly learns that as the Receiver, he must bear the entire world's pain, sadness, war, anguish, and loss. All of it.

It is the Receiver's job to carry all of this responsibility alone so the rest of the community never has to know it ever existed. The price of this freedom for the community, of course, is that they never know joy either.

Lois Lowry's *The Giver* is a morality tale, intended to make young people think about the role of pain and suffering in life. She wants her readers (both old and young) to think about what life would be like if we knew no pain, think about the price that painlessness would come with: the sacrifice of true joy, love, wonder, beauty, and the uniqueness among human beings and our experiences.

For Lowry, no amount of pain and suffering is worth the sacrifice of life's wonderfulness. They are all part of a meaningful human life.

Yet some Christian books on dating seem to take the opposite stance to Lowry's assessment of pain. They say you should not date because dating inevitably leads to pain and suffering. If you date before you have found *the one*, before you are ready to get married, you are only asking for it. Why set yourself up for heartbreak? Clearly heartbreak is God's way of telling us that dating before marriage is wrong and sinful. God punishes us with pain and suffering because by dating we go against what God wants for us.

This typical Christian perspective on why young people should not be dating echoes a typical warning that Donna's dad used to affectionately say to her when she was little and driving him crazy:

"Kid, you are cruisin' for a bruisin'."

In other words, young people are told that when they date, they are asking for it.

I (Donna) remember the time in college when my long-term boyfriend and I ended our relationship. He was my first love and we loved each other intensely. I was devastated over the loss of our relationship, and I sobbed more tears than both I and my friends thought possible to cry. I remember thinking to myself: Why did I open myself up to this hurt in the first place? How am I going to get through all of this pain?

While there were points when I thought that the hurt would never go away, it eventually waned. When it did, what was left in me was not the regret for having loved in the first place, but gratefulness that such an incredible possibility, the possibility of giving and receiving love, both its joys and struggles, had been bestowed on me. Looking back today I cherish that relationship, the first experience of loving and being loved, the intense highs and lows that result from loving intensely, as well as how much I learned about love in the process.

It's true that dating relationships do end and that these endings are not always easy. They are painful. They make us cry. They make us suffer to varying degrees depending on their significance to our lives. Endings are scary and make us feel helpless. We scream and yell about them and feel like the whole world is coming to an end. Even Jesus cried out on the cross.

Yet Jesus' willingness to undergo pain and death is at the very heart of salvation. At no point does he turn away from suffering (although he would have liked to as evidenced by his prayer in the Garden of Gethsemane). Because he does not reject suffering, he is able to restore life to people, heal wounds, forgive sins, and bring about the salvation of the world. If he had not been willing to suffer, none of this would have been possible.

Thus for us, we must realize that sometimes, out of endings come poetry, out of death, resurrection. Our very weakness and finitude are the grounds for us to realize the possible heights of our love for and appreciation of others. We learn that time and relationships are precious and that we should not take either for granted, that experiencing the joys of love are worth every tear we shed.

So the moral of the story is that the possibility of pain is not a good criteria for judging what should or should not be done. Often we suffer for doing what is right. Being open to the possibility of pain is necessary for us to have any hope of experiencing deep or sincere love. Yes, suffering, sadness, and loss are difficult and sometimes even devastating, but often in facing pain, we discover the deeper meaning and joys of life.

Facing the suffering that often comes with dating is not always easy. After all, none of us wants pain. Still, by being open to possible loss we are also open to love, and in this openness we grow spiritually.

Beginning Again Requires Faith

 One of our favorite movies about faith is *Field of Dreams*. The story is about a down-and-out farmer. Standing in his cornfield one evening, he hears a mysterious voice: "If you build it, he will come." The man has no idea where the voice is coming from, if it is his imagination or if it is real, if someone is playing a trick on him or if it is the voice of God. Yet he begins to hear the same instruction over and over again as he remains standing, perplexed, in his cornfield.

So what does he do in response to this voice? He begins a journey with no idea where it will lead. He eventually believes he must build a baseball diamond in his cornfield, takes the risk and builds it, earning himself ridicule because of its seeming absurdity. He leaps into the journey with his whole heart, convincing his family and eventually another unlikely companion to believe and join him in this leaping.

The result of his willingness to leap is magical, romantic, and moving. You, the viewer, walk away from the theater or turn off the television stunned, inspired, and reflective. You believe yourself that it was all worth it in the end — building the baseball diamond in the cornfield, as absurd as it may sound. You feel transformed, even if just for a moment, sharing in the magic of the story.

The farmer's leap of faith turns out to be a beautiful choice, even though it meant taking great risks on his part. You love him for believing, for his willingness to have faith. You love him for helping you overcome your own disbelief, if only for the duration of the story.

Leaps of faith are required of us in so many aspects of life. Every night when we go to bed we take a leap of faith that the sun will be there to greet us in the morning. With faith we get into the car every day believing that we will safely arrive at work. We have faith in our friends, that they will be loyal to us and supportive in times of need. You don't have to be a down-and-out farmer who builds a baseball diamond to have faith or to do some leaping — we just do not often reflect on how much leaping is required of us just to manage our everyday lives. Yet it turns out that faith is everywhere we turn.

Faith is especially necessary when we are dating, again.

St. John of the Cross, a sixteenth-century mystic, described a particularly difficult period in his journey toward God as "the dark night of the soul." John is not only beloved for telling his extraordinary experiences of the divine, but also for the way in which he described them — through both poetry and descriptive prose. According to John, "the dark night" is a profoundly intense and lonely time, when the soul experiences its "deepest poverty and wretchedness.... It feels within itself a profound emptiness and impoverishment."[23]

According to St. John, the dark night is a time in one's relationship with or journey to God when one believes that all hope of love from God is lost. The dark night of the soul is a time when one despairs and feels totally alone and abandoned. During the dark night, it is easy to lose hope of coming out the other side of this despair, of finding the right path again, and of being flooded by God's love once more. The dark night of the soul is a time on the journey where one's faith stumbles and threatens to melt away, a time where one's *will* to be on the journey seems lost.

During the aftermath of a breakup, we often become acquainted with what we could describe as our own "dark night," though perhaps not always as extreme as St. John has described it. The dark night is the loss of love. It is a loss of the will to keep loving. It is a being alone again after one has experienced the wonders of giving and receiving love. Once one knows love, it is all the more difficult to lose love. After love, it is so easy to believe that one will never be the beneficiary of love again. Love seems impossibly far away and out of reach. The dark night in dating also may involve a loss of hope in future romantic relationships, in others because they may have hurt us, or even in our capacity to be with others again in this type of relationship.

In describing the dark night of the soul, John describes a kind of temporary "breakup" in his relationship with God — or what John perceives to be a loss in his closeness to God. Though in reality God remains close, this perceived "breaking up" at the time feels permanent to John — hence his experience of deep despair and not being able to go on. The difference between John's "breakup" with God and our human relationships is, of course, that our breakups are often *not* temporary — that person we love usually does *not* remain close in a way we have merely

171

lost sight of. Our breakups are usually permanent — yet like John, we too see the morning after our dark nights of despair.

Throughout this book, we have described dating in many ways including as part of a journey and a spiritual shifting. We have discussed both the high and low points we face if we choose to date. We have talked often of the ways that dating can enrich us as individuals, in our capacity for loving relationships, in our understanding of what it means to be a Christian, and with regard to the role of spirituality in our lives. We have tried not to sugar-coat dating either, discussing the "thorns" that we face along the way, including the temporary quality that makes dating, *dating*.

There is no question that one of the most difficult moments we face in dating is the moment when we face the loss of the relationship. We have defended finitude in previous essays and we have talked of how we should not date just to avoid loneliness. Yet all of this advice does not take away the despair we feel, sometimes very, very intensely, at the loss of a relationship.

In dating, we face the dark night. The question becomes, how do we make it through? What do we need to make it out the other side? Why would we ever want to date again? Why not just save ourselves the despair?

It is this potential for loss and of grieving that is so often used as a deterrent for why people should not date. By never risking a relationship that might not last, we are somehow protecting ourselves. Yet upon further reflection, it becomes clear that protecting ourselves from loss is not a reason to abstain from dating. In fact, risk taking, *leap taking*, having faith, lies at the core of Christianity.

In reading the Gospels we see the confusion and despair of Jesus' followers when they face the reality that he would be killed. We see Jesus' own despair during his night in the garden. The enormous risks that these people took by following and believing

172

in Jesus seem to come to nothing at his death. Yet his death is not the end — there is, instead, a new beginning, a resurrection.

St. John of the Cross tells us that though in the dark night we encounter despair, it only makes the reencountering of love all the sweeter. In the reencountering we realize that even in our moments of despair we are never really alone.

The dark night, the loss and the grieving, even the experience of disbelief, are moments on our spiritual journeys. We should not run from them, but face them and move through them because there is another side. The other side turns out to be worth the risk.

Risking, stumbling, leaping, and rejoicing when we have righted ourselves again is what God calls us to in our spiritual life. Since dating can be an important part of our spiritual life, dating means taking similar chances. If we are to date, we must risk love, not just once but again and again.

As C. S. Lewis said, "The only place outside of Heaven where you can be perfectly safe from all the dangers and perturbations of love is Hell."[24] We don't live in either heaven or hell. We live on earth, and if we are to love in the here and now, we must take the risk that we may lose this love. Even though the risk of loss is high in dating, it is possible not only to survive it but also to come out of it better able and more open to loving again.

Why Loving Matters

 We are all probably familiar with the basic plot line of Robert Louis Stevenson's *The Strange Case of Dr. Jekyll and Mr. Hyde.* Dr. Jekyll is a decent fellow who drinks a potion that turns him into the evil Mr. Hyde. Most likely we have seen this idea played with in various television show or movies. In the Looney Tunes version, either Bugs Bunny drinks the potion which turns him into a monster that scares Elmer Fudd, or Tweety drinks it and scares away Sylvester.

Ha, ha, it is all in good fun, right?

The story by Stevenson was originally written as a horror piece. Many people assumed it was scary because the good Dr. Jekyll is really the bad Mr. Hyde. The true horror of the story, however, is different. It starts when Dr. Jekyll begins to wake up as Mr. Hyde without drinking the transformation potion. He begins to lose control over himself. He no longer wants to be Hyde but continually finds himself turning into him. Jekyll is forced to stay near his lab so that he can quickly take the potion that causes him to revert back.

The horror increases when Jekyll starts to run out of the antidote and cannot replicate the original formula. Jekyll keeps turning into Hyde and the change starts to happen more frequently and last longer. In the end, Jekyll kills himself realizing that he is about to permanently become Hyde.

This tragic situation is exacerbated by the psychological horror that Jekyll discovers. Initially Jekyll thinks of Hyde as a separate person. Whatever the doctor does as Hyde only affects Hyde. Jekyll believes that he can take the potion that reverts him back to himself and never suffer the repercussions of Hyde's actions. Jekyll believes this until Hyde starts to appear on his own without the transformation potion. It turns out that what Jekyll does as Hyde does affect Jekyll. As a matter of fact, each time Jekyll becomes Hyde, he unknowingly gave strength to the Hyde persona. Eventually Hyde becomes so strong that Jekyll can do nothing to stop him.

The horror is not that Jekyll is Hyde but that Jekyll cannot stop becoming Hyde. In the end, he becomes Hyde not because he wanted to or because he made a conscious decision to — he always thought the transformation could be controlled through the potion. He becomes Hyde because it was the inevitable consequence of his decisions. Each decision made Jekyll into more of Hyde. Before Jekyll realized what was going on, he could not help but become Hyde in his entire being.

Why are we writing so much about a scary story from the 1800s? In addition to being an exciting and fun read, *The Strange Case of Dr. Jekyll and Mr. Hyde* is a careful study of human psychology. It shows how we shape ourselves through our actions. All our actions have consequences — some we see, others we do not. Each one leads to the shaping of the individual we are to become. It can be horrible like the case of Dr. Jekyll, but it can also be wonderful. We can approach sainthood without even realizing it just by doing our daily tasks well.

This, we believe, is what happened to Mother Teresa. When we both were in graduate school, Mother Teresa came to our campus for the induction of new sisters into her order. During one of these visits, a man was walking up the center aisle of the church and fell down. Mother Teresa was the first there and the first to help him up. Everyone was moved, and people talked about it for days. One of our professors pointed out that the truly moving aspect about Mother Teresa was not that she helped the guy up — this was just one act — but that she had been doing these same types of actions for almost her entire life. She helped because she had become the kind of person that could do nothing else.

Perhaps we need a new story called *The Strange Case of Mother Teresa and Saint Teresa.*

Practice, this is the key. Through his decisions, Dr. Jekyll was "practicing" to become Hyde. Through her decisions, Mother Teresa was "practicing" to become a saint.

We must practice what we want to become.

The kind of practice we do in life, though, is slightly different than, say, practicing a sport or music. With sports or music, the practice prepares you for the game or the concert. With ourselves, our practice is our lives. It is comparable to learning to play a sport or an instrument *during* a game or concert. Yet as humans we cannot withdraw from living to practice our actions, we must practice while we are playing and the playing never stops.

What should we practice to become?

Jesus gives his followers two rules. (Only two?! It seems we hear so many more coming from the pulpit.) Jesus' rules were love God and love your neighbor (Matthew 22:37–39). So all believers are supposed to become creatures of love. They are called to love God, the enemy, the stranger, the neighbor, and even the self. If this is who we are to become, how do we practice it? How do we learn to love the enemy, stranger, and neighbor?

Womanist theologian bell hooks argues that the only way to practice loving is through committed and mutual relationships. hooks studies this practice in the black community. She believes that the practice of respectful, mutual, loving relationships is not the norm among blacks. Rather, one all too frequently finds the denigration of love, despair about the possibility of love, and even violence and unfaithfulness that is erroneously called love.

She believes that it is only through loving and mutual relationships that the situation can improve. If people practice these relationships, they will not only transform themselves but the communities in which they live. As hooks puts it, "We cannot effectively resist domination if our efforts to create meaningful, lasting personal and social change are not grounded in a love ethic."[25] The "love ethic" is loving relationships and the foundation for becoming a people and a community that loves.

The beauty of hooks's insight is that it is not only applicable to the black community but to all people. If we, no matter who we are, do not practice loving relationships, we will not become the people of love that God calls us to be. The loving relationships of which we speak could take the form of friendship or marriage. We, however, are interested in dating. Since a loving relationship is also the hoped-for foundation of a dating relationship, dating can be understood as practicing love as well. As stated earlier, it is this practice that enables us to become a people of love.

Given all of what we have said, why, then, does loving matter?

Initially it matters because God calls us to love. Hence, we should always be concerned about responding to this call. hooks pointed out that love can rebuild and reform communities. The examples of Mother Teresa and Dr. Jekyll show us that love (or the lack thereof) can form who we are as people. There are many ways we can practice love, but one way is dating. Thus, for those who date — whether Christian, spiritual, or both — and for those who are concerned with their own character and the good of community, loving is essential. Only if we approach our dating relationships with love will we become a people and a community that genuinely loves.

The goodness of the world depends on loving, and this is why loving matters.

This is also why dating matters — in dating, love is practiced.

A Few Closing Thoughts

If you told us when we began our friendship that we would end up writing a book together, we never would have believed you. Our common interests were school and food. We only haphazardly stumbled onto the topic of dating and how spirituality, theology, and dating are related. The more we talked about it and shared our ideas with other people, the more we felt we needed to do something. We wanted to work to "save" dating.

What does it mean to "save" dating? The verb to save usually has two connotations: to save from and to save for. For Christians, we are saved from sin and for life with God. When we talk about saving dating, we talk about saving dating *from* culture's superficial understanding of dating and some Christians' disdain for it, and *for* its role in our spiritual lives.

This whole book has been working toward this "saving." We have written on dozens of topics — from how dating strengthens our spiritual life to why we all want movie love to the value of kissing — and now we have come to the end of the book. We proposed in the essay "Breaking Up Is Not a Failure" that endings are not evil or sinful but are part of living in the material world and part of human finitude. In "So You're a Born-Again Virgin," we suggested that when considering past experiences we should not bury the experiences but reflect on them in order to grow in our lives today.

Working on this book has been a lot like dating. We both started out in extreme excitement over the idea of working together. We were even more delighted when The Crossroad Publishing Company agreed to publish this book. After this initial exhilaration wore off, we had the task of sitting down and writing the book. Like any good relationship, each essay was work but a work that resulted in happiness.

At times, we got along great, and at other times we disagreed. We didn't ever fight, which was a bit of a surprise considering some of our differences, but we did have to apologize to one another a few times.

Now that this book is done, we need to follow our own advice: we need to reflect on what we have written. While this reflection will continue for years to come, we already have some ideas of where to start. What follows is what we think are some of our most important ideas. They are found not in just one essay but throughout the book.

Idea 1: Spirituality is inextricably linked to the physical world.

Our spirituality is not something apart from our bodies but is bound to them. If we neglect our body, our spiritual life, or their connection, we disregard a genuine part of our human existence.

All of our activities, then, should contribute to our whole selves, physical and spiritual. Since dating is an activity in this world, an activity that many of us engage in and some of us over a long period of time, we need to see its connection to our souls. We need to see how it impacts our lives, our *whole* lives. We need to understand dating so that we date in such a way that it makes us better people and, if we are Christian, draws us closer to God.

Idea 2: The most important commandments are to love God and love your neighbor.

So often our culture beckons us to focus on the superficial. We are told to prize a particular type of clothes, car, soap, or television show. Loving God, however, calls us away from evaluating the world we live in by particular brand names. We are to love something immanent to yet also beyond our culture, our world, and ourselves, something we often term goodness, truth, or beauty.

179

The love of God both reminds us of these values and moves us to hold them dear.

Christianity also emphasizes the love of neighbor. We are to practice our love by connecting to other people. Sometimes this is helping the stranger; sometimes this is helping the friend. We maintain that this practice can be done in dating as well. So while we need remember that there is a reality beyond this world, we also need to be reminded of our responsibilities for loving in this world.

If we apply these two commandments to dating, we need to remember that everything that we hear from culture is not the be all and end all and that genuinely loving another is an integral part of being a Christian and a human person in general. Moreover, we need to respect the value of each person we date and treat him or her in a loving manner.

Idea 3: Finitude, either in our lives or in dating relationships, is not evil.

Human life ends. Dating relationships end. These endings do cause great sorrow in our lives. Yet they are not evil. The fact that we die does not make life evil; the fact that relationships end does not make dating evil. In dating, what is evil is if part of the relationship involves physical, mental, or spiritual abuse. Abuse is not an intrinsic part nor should it ever be an aspect of a romantic relationship, whether finite or lifelong.

Idea 4: Dating is like a clue to a mystery.

We spent a lot of time with this metaphor. We claimed that dating can be an important part of being alive. In dating, we meet and come to love new and different people. These people, regardless of whether we stay with them or break up with them, lead us to discoveries about the world, other people, and ourselves. These discoveries reveal some of the mysteries to living.

If you are a Christian, the metaphor is expanded because the mystery that dating helps you to understand is not just life here on earth but also eternal life. Dating is a loving relationship, and it is love that enables us to understand God better and our response to this Being who loves us.

Idea 5: Others are gifts.

If dating is like a clue to a mystery, we should view dating in a positive light. We need the clues to solve the mystery. Part of viewing dating this way is viewing other people as gifts. We are not to be afraid of them because they might lead us astray or corrupt us. We must see other people as good and possible mediators of God's grace. Jesus sees others in this light and calls us to do likewise: whatever you do to someone else you do to God.

True, we are not called to date everyone that comes along, but then all gifts are not the same. Just as we have Christmas, birthday, and anniversary gifts, so too we have people who are our family, our friends, and sometimes our romantic interest. They are different, even though they are all gifts. Dating someone is seeing her or him as a particular type of gift.

Idea 6: Sexuality is important.

One corollary of seeing people as gift is seeing sexuality as positive. So often sex is thought of as the greatest sin. Since sexual activity usually happens between two people, the condemnation of sex becomes a fear of other people. If, however, we see sexuality as something good, it strengthens our view of other people as good. In addition, *good* sexual expression in dating — physical expression that stems from a loving relationship — reemphasizes the fact that our physical existence is intimately connected to our spiritual existence.

Idea 7: Diversity is important for human flourishing.

Human beings are relational creatures. We flourish in good relationships and there are diverse types of dating relationships. Individuals need people who are different from them to help them grow. God also seems to value difference. The divine is expressed through the diversity we encounter in our lives.

When we date, we date people who are different than we are. They cannot only reinforce our beliefs but also challenge us with their own. Both are good, both are necessary, and both only come because there is a diversity of people in the world.

Idea 8: Dating is an option not the option.

Throughout this book, we have described dating in various ways. We have said that it is more than friendship and less than marriage, a relationship that includes physical, emotional, and spiritual dimensions. It can be as short as one night out or as long as several years, and it usually does not evolve into marriage — that is what makes it dating, not courtship. Dating can be valuable to our human and religious flourishing. Yet we are just pointing out one way. Other options — like not dating — may lead to similar thriving in the physical and spiritual world.

These are some of the main reflections we take with us from our writing. We're sure that we will continue to reflect on and add to them throughout the years. We believe that these are important aspects of any attempt to "save the date" and hope that they prove of assistance for you.

Thanks for listening.

Notes

1. C. S. Lewis, *The Screwtape Letters* (New York: Macmillan, 1982), 20.

2. Vincent Genovesi, *In Pursuit of Love: Catholic Morality and Human Sexuality* (Collegeville, Minn.: Liturgical Press, 1996), 178.

3. Robert Johnson, "Beyond Romance to Human Love," *Perspectives on Marriage: A Reader*, 2d ed., Kieran Scott and Michael Warren, eds. (Oxford University Press, 2001), 169–76.

4. Aristotle, *Nicomachean Ethics*, 2.1.

5. Bernard Lonergan, *Method in Theology* (Toronto: University of Toronto Press, 1994), 105.

6. "Choosing Virginity," *Newsweek*, December 9, 2002, 61.

7. At a talk on the ethics and spirituality of dating we gave at the Mid-Atlantic Regional Conference for the American Academy of Religion (AAR) in 2002, Dr. Robert Barry was asked by the AAR to give a response to the issues we raised in our talk. His reply to the difficult issue of determining what level of sexual activity in a dating relationship is permissible was to ask whether we could understand the concept of chastity as it would apply in a dating relationship. We thought that he raised an interesting question and decided to try to address it more fully in one of our essays here.

8. Dorothee Soelle with Shirley A. Cloyes, *To Work and to Love: A Theology of Creation* (Philadelphia: Fortress Press, 1984), 144.

9. Elisabeth Moltmann-Wendel, *I Am My Body: A Theology of Embodiment* (New York: Continuum, 1995), 60–65.

10. Grace Jantzen, *Power, Gender, and Christian Mysticism* (New York: Cambridge University Press, 1995), 149.

11. Ibid., 135.

12. Thomas Aquinas, *Summa Contra Gentiles*, 2.45.2.

13. James Fowler, *Stages of Faith: The Psychology of Human Development and the Quest for Meaning* (San Francisco: HarperSanFrancisco, 1981), 4.

14. Ibid., 76–77, 174–83.

15. John Paul II, *Familiaris Consortio*, 78.

16. Sharon Parks, *Big Questions, Worthy Dreams: Mentoring Young Adults in Their Search for Meaning, Purpose, and Faith* (San Francisco: Jossey-Bass, 2000), 27–31.

17. C. S. Lewis, *The Great Divorce* (San Francisco: HarperCollins, 2001), 2.

18. Ibid., 3.

19. Dorothy Day, *The Long Loneliness* (San Francisco: HarperSanFrancisco, 1997), 286.

20. Ibid., 285.

21. Grace Jantzen, *Becoming Divine: Toward a Feminist Philosophy of Religion* (Bloomington: Indiana University Press, 1999), 156–70.

22. Dorothy Sayers, "Problem Picture," *The Whimsical Christian* (New York: Collier Books, 1987), 133.

23. St. John of the Cross, *Dark Night of the Soul*, trans. and ed. E. Allison Peers (New York: Doubleday, 1990), 106.

24. C. S. Lewis, *The Four Loves* (New York: Harvest/HBJ Books, 1960), 169.

25. bell hooks, *Salvation: Black People and Love* (New York: HarperCollins, 2001), xxiv.

Bibliography

Aquinas, Thomas. *Summa Contra Gentiles.* Trans. Anton C. Pegis. Notre Dame, Ind.: University of Notre Dame Press, 1975.

Aristotle. *Nicomachean Ethics.* Trans. Martin Ostwald. New York: Macmillan, 1962.

Austen, Jane. *Pride and Prejudice.* New York: Bantam Books, 1981.

Browne, Joy. *Dating for Dummies.* Philadelphia: Running Press, 1997.

"Choosing Virginity." *Newsweek.* December 9, 2002, 61.

Day, Dorothy. *The Long Loneliness.* San Francisco: HarperSanFrancisco, 1997.

Fein, Ellen, and Sherrie Schneider. *The Rules: Time Tested Secrets for Capturing the Heart of Mr. Right.* New York: Pocket Books, 2002.

Fowler, James. *Stages of Faith: The Psychology of Human Development and the Quest for Meaning.* San Francisco: HarperSanFrancisco, 1981.

Genovesi, Vincent. *In Pursuit of Love: Catholic Morality and Human Sexuality.* Collegeville, Minn.: Liturgical Press, 1996.

Gilligan, Carol. *In a Different Voice: Psychological Theory and Women's Development.* Cambridge, Mass.: Harvard University Press, 1993.

Gray, John. *Men Are from Mars, Women Are from Venus: A Practical Guide for Improving Communication and Getting What You Want in Your Relationships.* New York: HarperCollins, 1992.

Gutiérrez, Gustavo. *A Theology of Liberation.* Trans. Sr. Caridad Inda and John Eagleson. Maryknoll, N.Y.: Orbis Books, 1988.

Harris, Joshua. *I Kissed Dating Goodbye.* Sisters, Ore.: Multnomah, 1999.

hooks, bell. *Salvation: Black People and Love.* New York: HarperCollins, 2001.

Jantzen, Grace. *Becoming Divine: Toward a Feminist Philosophy of Religion.* Bloomington: Indiana University Press, 1999.

———. *Power, Gender, and Christian Mysticism.* New York: Cambridge University Press, 1995.

John of the Cross, St. *Dark Night of the Soul.* Trans. E. Allison Peers. New York: Doubleday, 1990.

John Paul II. *Familiaris Consortio: The Role of the Christian Family in the Modern World.* Boston: Pauline Books & Media, 1997.

Johnson, Robert. "Beyond Romance to Human Love." In *Perspective on Marriage: A Reader.* 2d ed. Ed. Kieran Scott and Michael Warren. Oxford University Press, 2001.

Kaplan, Alexandra G., Jean Baker Miller, Iren Stiver, Janet L. Surrey, Judith V. Jordan, and Irene Pierce Stiver. *Women's Growth in Connection: Writings from the Stone Center.* New York: Guilford Press, 1991.

Kuriansky, Judy. *The Complete Idiot's Guide to Dating.* New York: Macmillan Publishing USA, 1998.

Laurie, Greg. *God's Design for Christian Dating.* Eugene, Ore.: Harvest House, 1983.

Lewis, C. S. *The Four Loves.* New York: Harvest/HBJ Books, 1960.

———. *The Great Divorce.* San Francisco: HarperCollins, 2001.

———. *The Screwtape Letters.* New York: Macmillan, 1982.

Lonergan, Bernard. *Method in Theology.* Toronto: University of Toronto Press, 1994.

Lowry, Lois. *The Giver.* Boston: Houghton Mifflin, 2002

Moltmann-Wendel, Elisabeth. *I Am My Body: A Theology of Embodiment.* New York: Continuum, 1995.

Moore, Stephanie. *Staying Pure.* Chicago: Moody Press, 2000.

Parks, Sharon. *Big Questions, Worthy Dreams: Mentoring Young Adults in Their Search for Meaning, Purpose, and Faith.* San Francisco: Jossey-Bass, 2000.

Piven, Joshua, Jennifer Worick, Brenda Brown, and David Borgenicht. *The Worst-Case Scenario Survival Handbook: Dating and Sex.* San Francisco: Chronicle Books, 2001.

Pullman, Philip. *His Dark Materials Trilogy.* New York: Knopf, 2002.

Sayers, Dorothy. "Problem Picture." *The Whimsical Christian.* New York: Collier Books, 1987.

Soelle, Dorothee, with Shirley A. Cloyes. *To Work and to Love: A Theology of Creation.* Philadelphia: Fortress Press, 1984.

Stevenson, Robert Louis. *The Strange Case of Dr. Jekyll and Mr. Hyde.* New York: Aeonian Press, 1978.

St. James, Rebecca, and Dale Reeves. *Wait for Me: The Beauty of Sexual Purity.* Nashville: Thomas Nelson, 1997.

Wentworth, Theodore, with Lexi von Welanetz. *Build a Better Spouse Trap.* New York: M. Evans, 2002.

West, Christopher. *The Good News about Sex and Marriage.* Ann Arbor, Mich.: Servant Publications, 2000.

Why We Are Thankful
for Our Relationships
(aka Acknowledgments)

There are several people we would like to thank together. Gwendolin Herder, thank you for taking a risk on our dating book. Jean Blomquist, your suggestions on the manuscript were really helpful. Stephen Happel, Cynthia Crysdale, Margaret Kelleher, and Joseph Komonchak, our graduate school professors from the Catholic University of America, we are extremely thankful for your role in our academic formation and subsequent encouragement.

Also, thank you, Roy M. Carlisle. We realized pretty early on how lucky we were to have you as our editor. Your encouragement, enthusiasm, criticisms, mentoring, and professional expertise made this book a reality. We could not have completed it without you. And on top of all that, you took us to a yummy dinner.

In addition, Jason would like to thank...

Friends are indispensable for almost anything we do. In writing, my friends have helped me in ways untold — from supporting me and joking with me to proofreading for me and giving me ideas. To all my friends, I would like to extend my thanks, but I do have a few in particular that I would like to mention. To Jon Gross, you suck. To Amy Gross, you know Jon has bad genes, don't you? To Tod Donhauser and Louise Hjort, seriously, when are you two getting married? To Chris and Deb, I know you wanted a book jacket blurb but all I could get you was an essay. To Mike and Karen O'Brien, thanks for the prayers. To Fred and Lynda Poling, thanks for being my normal friends. To Colleen Durkin, thanks for your comments and "scary feet, scary feet." To Donna, what a strange, tripped-out, truly enriching, and exciting friendship we've had. Can you believe we wrote a book together?

Although I have not been teaching long, my colleagues have been crucial in supporting and encouraging me. I would especially like to thank Geof Grubb and Sr. Shannon Schrein of Lourdes College. You two have supported this project in spirit and gone out of your way to promote it on and off campus. I look forward to working with you for many years. I would also like to thank Bob Draghi of Marymount University for mentoring me in my first years as a professor.

I must also thank Fred and Carol deRosset. God has worked through you to get to me. This book is in part the fruit of that grace. I hope both of you continue to enrich the lives of people around you.

Without my family, I would not have the blessed life I have now. Mom and Dad, there is no way to ever thank you enough for all that you have given me. Todd and Angel, thank you for being family and friends. Nanny, thank you for being a wonderful grandmother. I hope the book makes you proud. Papaw, I wish you had lived to see the publication of this book.

My last thanks goes to Kelly, my six-year girlfriend and now wife. I wish I had the space to detail all the ways you have loved me well. I do not, so I will just mention the most important. Because of you, I have grown as a person, a writer, a son, and a friend. I have grown with you and, with your support, with all of my friends. All I can say in return is, "Praise the Lord for Dapple things."

Finally, Donna would like to thank . . .

As with Jason, relationships are the central, sustaining force in my life. There are many without which this book would not have come to pass.

To Margaret and Kylie — you have been so incredibly supportive throughout my year of writing this book. What would I do without you continuously reminding me of all my past dates? To Bridget see above note to M and K and thanks for listening over the years. To Heather, thank you for your unconditional love and friendship, for introducing me to my future, and for being the most courageous mommy I know. Layton, you are one of the most supportive and wonderful friends I have ever had. That goes for you too, Shelley — and I can't wait to visit again. To Ridgeway, I love you despite that whole religion thing (you know what I'm talking about). To Jonathan, sorry I threw that shoe, and by the way, this book is like one great big relationship talk, isn't it? Also, to Julie, Kaitlin, Andrea, Suzan, Susie, and Vidya — thank you for the friendship and support. To Dr. Stephen and Professor Ambrosio, you give me something to aspire to — thank you. To Gene Monterastelli, my "funky-juggling-youth-minister" friend — thank you for your presence in my life, your humor, the juggling lessons, and advice on this book.

To Kristen Lynaugh — little did I know what you would become in my life — like a sister. Thank you for your dedication, laughter, spiritual guidance and faith, for being a mentor, and for all those yummy Jell-O pies you leave in my fridge. And by the way, thank God for all those weird things we did as kids — I've never laughed so hard in my life!

To Jason (aka J), I am thankful to call you friend and share such an incredible experience with you in writing this book. You are the bridesmaid I always dreamed about! Need I say more?

To Mom and Dad, so in retrospect, I probably should not have made that comparison between Santa Claus and God back in college. I had decided I was an atheist, OK? Thank you for giving me a tradition to struggle with — who would have thought — a Ph.D. in religion!

To my students, past and present, you inspire and make my work the rich journey that it is — thank you for teaching me over the years. I would like to mention a few by name: Dave Gilbertson, all my staff from the "West Side" at Georgetown, Nancy Moser, and Heath Carter, and, of course, Carlyle SAB 02-03. Finally, to the students of New York University InterVarsity and in particular, Cara Gouldey — thank you for reading and for all the advice!

Thank you to Java n Jazz for the great coffee and space to write the book.

Last but certainly not least, to Josh, the rock star in my life. There are not enough pages in this book to contain all of my thanks and appreciation — good thing I have a lifetime for that. Without you, your support, love, encouragement, humor, those indispensable comments on the book, innumerable glasses of water, your kindness throughout the "great tooth caper," and your willingness to suffer through Trading Spaces despite it all, I could not have made it through this year. Can you believe there was a time when we were just friends?

And to our future readers — thank you for giving this book a chance.

About the Authors

Jason King was raised in Berea, Kentucky. After college, he lived for a year in Chicago before moving to Washington, D.C., for graduate school. He spent several years playing soccer, dating, and hanging out with his friends while trying to complete his Ph.D. When he graduated, he took a full-time job at Lourdes College in Ohio. He is now teaching some wonderful students, enjoying his new colleagues, and splitting his life between research and cable TV.

Donna Freitas grew up in the little state that could: Rhode Island. After spending her childhood as a resident beach bum and attending more proms than she would like to admit, Donna moved to Washington, D.C., to attend Georgetown University. There she discovered her love of asking questions, her desire to teach, and the sneaking suspicion she would have to get her Ph.D. at some point. Her suspicions were correct, and in 2002 she graduated from Catholic University with a Ph.D. in Religious Studies. Since college and while working on her degree, Donna has held a multitude of student-focused positions, at the Close Up Foundation, in the Departments of Residence Life and Campus Ministry at Georgetown University, as well as in Residence Life at New York University. She is currently full-time faculty at St. Michael's College in Burlington, Vermont, teaching, writing, drinking lots of coffee to stay warm, and keeping up with her favorite musician, Josh Dodes.